AF569964

One Year with Covid-19

edited by Christian Ewert & Lea Heyne

Bibliografische Information der Deutschen Nationalbibliothek
Die Deutsche Nationalbibliothek verzeichnet diese Publikation in der Deutschen Nationalbibliografie; detaillierte bibliografische Daten sind im Internet über http://dnb.d-nb.de abrufbar

The views expressed in this book reflect the personal opinions of their respective authors

DemocracyNet is a non-profit organization located in Switzerland
https://democracynet.eu
info@democracynet.eu

Layout: Christian Ewert
Cover picture: Lea Heyne

Herstellung und Verlag: BoD – Books on Demand, Norderstedt

ISBN: 978-3-75340-228-4

Content

– B –

Politische Implikationen | Les implications politiques
Implicazioni politiche | Political implications

– C –

Länderberichte | Rapports par pays
Relazioni sui paesi | Country reports

Appendix

Die Einleitung

Lea Heyne & Christian Ewert

Ende Dezember 2019 tauchten in den Medien die ersten Meldungen über das Auftreten einer «neuen Lungenkrankheit» in Wuhan, China auf. Ab Januar 2020 wurden die Fälle langsam zahlreicher, breiteten sich auch ausserhalb von China aus, und die Krankheit bekam einen Namen: Covid-19. Am 11. März 2020 erklärte die Weltgesundheitsorganisation (WHO) Covid-19 schliesslich zur Pandemie, seitdem ist kein Tag vergangen, an dem Covid-19 nicht die Schlagzeilen und unser Alltagsleben dominiert.

Auch unsere politischen Systeme haben durch diese Pandemie einen Schock erlitten. Die drohende Überforderung der Gesundheitssysteme setzte demokratische Regierungen unter akuten Zugzwang, und führte zu Massnahmen, die wir noch kurz zuvor für unmöglich gehalten hätten – Lockdowns, Ausgangsbeschränkungen, Schulschliessungen, Maskenpflicht. Damit ist das vergangene Jahr auch aus demokratischer Sicht eine Ausnahmeerscheinung. Und obwohl die Pandemie bei weitem noch nicht vorbei ist, scheint es uns nun ein guter Anlass, um ein erstes Fazit zu ziehen: Wie hat ein Jahr Covid-19 unsere Demokratie verändert? Die Idee hinter diesem Buch ist denkbar einfach: Wir haben Demokratie-Forschende aus verschiedensten Fachrichtungen und Ländern gefragt, welche Implikationen sich nach einem Jahr mit Covid-19 für die Demokratie ergeben haben. Welche Herausforderungen und Chancen stellt Covid-19 für demokratische Repräsentation, Partizipation und Entscheidungsfindung? Welche Schwachstellen und Stärken einzelner Länder wurden durch die Pandemie offengelegt?

Unser Ziel war es von Anfang an, ein breites Publikum anzusprechen. Entsprechend sind die 26 Beiträge sehr kurz gehalten und in den Sprachen Deutsch, Französisch, Italienisch und Englisch geschrieben. Das Buch setzt drei Schwerpunkte und ist daher in drei Teile gegliedert: soziale Implikationen, politische Implikationen und länderspezifische Berichte. Wir hoffen, zum Nachdenken und gemeinsam Diskutieren anzuregen.

L’introduction

Lea Heyne & Christian Ewert

Fin décembre 2019, les premiers reportages concernant l’émergence d’une « nouvelle maladie pulmonaire » à Wuhan, en Chine, sont apparus dans les médias. À partir de janvier 2020, les cas ont lentement augmenté en nombre, se répandant en dehors de la Chine, et la maladie a reçu un nom : la Covid-19. Le 11 mars 2020, l’Organisation mondiale de la santé (OMS) a finalement déclaré que la Covid-19 constituait une pandémie ; depuis lors, pas un jour ne s’est écoulé sans que la pandémie ne fasse les gros titres et ne domine notre vie quotidienne.

Nos systèmes politiques ont eux aussi subi un choc. La menace de la surcharge des systèmes de santé a mis les gouvernements démocratiques sous forte pression et a conduit à des mesures que nous aurions crues impossibles peu de temps auparavant – confinement, couvre-feu, fermeture des écoles, obligation de port du masque. L’année écoulée est donc également exceptionnelle du point de vue démocratique. Et bien que la pandémie soit loin d’être terminée, il nous semble qu’il s’agit du bon moment pour tirer de premières conclusions : comment une année de Covid-19 a-t-elle changé notre démocratie ? L’idée derrière ce livre est très simple : nous nous sommes adressés à des chercheuses et chercheurs s’intéressant à la démocratie et issus d’un large éventail de disciplines et de pays, et nous leur avons demandé quelles étaient les implications d’une année de pandémie de Covid-19 pour la démocratie. Quels sont les défis et les opportunités créés par la Covid-19 pour la représentation démocratique, la participation et la prise de décision ? Quelles faiblesses et forces des différents pays la pandémie a-t-elle exposées ?

Dès le départ, notre objectif était de nous adresser à un large public. Les 26 contributions sont donc très brèves et rédigées en allemand, français, italien et anglais. Le livre se concentre sur trois domaines principaux et est donc divisé en trois parties : les implications sociales, les implications politiques et les implications dans différents pays. Nous espérons ainsi stimuler la réflexion et les discussions communes.

L'introduzione

Lea Heyne & Christian Ewert

A fine dicembre 2019 sono apparse sui media le prime notizie di una «nuova malattia polmonare» a Wuhan, in Cina. A partire da gennaio 2020 i casi sono lentamente aumentati, diffondendosi al di fuori della Cina, e alla malattia è stato infine dato un nome: Covid-19. L'11 marzo 2020 l'Organizzazione Mondiale della Sanità (OMS) ha dichiarato il Covid-19 una pandemia. Da allora non è passato un giorno senza che il Covid-19 dominasse i titoli di giornale e la nostra vita quotidiana.

I nostri sistemi politici sono stati scossi da questa pandemia. Il pericolo di un sovraccarico del sistema sanitario ha messo sotto forte pressione i governi democratici, portando all'introduzione di misure ritenute impossibili fino a poco tempo prima: lockdown, coprifuoco, chiusura delle scuole, obbligo della mascherina. Tutto ciò ha reso il 2020 un anno straordinario, anche dal punto di vista democratico. E anche se la pandemia è tutt'altro che finita, ci sembra che questo sia un buon momento per trarre delle prime conclusioni: com'è cambiata la democrazia dopo un anno di Covid-19? L'idea alla base di questo libro è molto semplice: abbiamo chiesto a ricercatrici e ricercatori provenienti da vari ambiti e paesi quali fossero secondo loro le implicazioni per la democrazia dopo un anno di Covid-19. Quali sfide e opportunità pone il Covid-19 per la rappresentanza, la partecipazione e il processo decisionale? Quali punti deboli e punti di forza sono venuti alla luce durante la pandemia nei singoli paesi?

Il nostro obiettivo è di rivolgerci ad un vasto pubblico. Per questo motivo tutti i 26 contributi sono molto brevi e sono scritti in tedesco, francese, italiano o inglese. Il libro si concentra su tre tematiche chiave ed è quindi diviso in tre parti: impatto sociale, implicazioni politiche e relazioni sui paesi. Speriamo di stimolare la riflessione dei nostri lettori ed una più ampia discussione pubblica.

The introduction

Lea Heyne & Christian Ewert

In late December 2019, the first reports of the emergence of a "new lung disease" in Wuhan, China appeared in the media. Starting in January 2020, cases slowly became more numerous, spreading outside of China, and the disease was given a name: Covid-19. On March 11, 2020, the World Health Organization (WHO) finally declared Covid-19 a pandemic; since then, not a day has gone by without Covid-19 dominating the headlines and our daily lives.

Our political systems have also been shocked by this pandemic. The threat of overstretching health systems put democratic governments under acute pressure to act, and led to measures we would have thought impossible just a short time before - lockdowns, curfews, school closures, mandatory masking. This makes the past year an exceptional one, even from a democratic perspective. And although the pandemic is far from over, it seems to us that now is a good time to draw an initial conclusion: how has one year of Covid-19 changed our democracy? The idea behind this book is very simple: we asked democracy researchers from a wide range of disciplines and countries what the implications are for democracy after one year with Covid-19. What challenges and opportunities does Covid-19 pose for democratic representation, participation, and decision-making? What weaknesses and strengths of individual countries have been exposed by the pandemic?

From the beginning, our goal was to address a broad audience. Accordingly, the 26 contributions are very brief and written in German, French, Italian and English. The book focuses on three main areas and is thus divided into three parts: social implications, political implications and country-specific reports. We hope to stimulate reflection and joint discussions.

– A –

Soziale Implikationen
Les implications sociales
Impatto sociale
Social implications

Soziale Implikationen

Welche Implikationen hat Covid-19 auf die Gesellschaft? Auf das Pflegepersonal, auf alte Menschen und andere besonders gefährdete Personen, auf Schulen? Wie verändert sich das Verhältnis zwischen Staat und Gesellschaft, und wie verändert sich die Kommunikation zwischen Staat und Gesellschaft?

Les implications sociales

Quelles sont les implications de la Covid-19 pour la société ? Pour le personnel soignant, les personnes âgées et les autres personnes particulièrement vulnérables, pour les écoles ? Comment la relation entre l'État et la société change-t-elle, et comment la communication entre l'État et la société se modifie-t-elle ?

Impatto sociale

Quali sono le implicazioni del Covid-19 per la società? Ad esempio, per il personale di assistenza, per gli anziani e altre persone particolarmente vulnerabili, per le scuole? Come cambiano il rapporto e la comunicazione tra Stato e società?

Social implications

What are the implications of Covid-19 for society? For the nursing staff, for the elderly and other particularly vulnerable people, for schools? How does the relationship between state and society change, and how does communication between state and society change?

1) L'accès aux soins en temps de crise : un déséquilibre démocratique

Maxime G. Zermatten & Christian Ewert

La crise sanitaire due au nouveau coronavirus 2019 (SARS-CoV-2) causant la maladie à coronavirus 2019 (Covid-19) a ébranlé le monde entier. Les pays dits développés se caractérisant par une forme de démocratie moderne se sont retrouvés face à une maladie inconnue et à un défi de taille : assurer, malgré un afflux massif de malades, des soins de qualité pour tous. « Pour tous » signifie que chaque être humain malade de la Covid-19, mais aussi que chaque être humain malade de n'importe quelle autre maladie ait accès à un traitement répondant aux standards de qualité habituels. En effet, le principe de démocratie moderne est indissociable de l'égalité de chaque être humain, telle qu'énoncée depuis la Déclaration des droits de l'homme et du citoyen, renouvelée dans la Déclaration universelle des droits de l'homme et reprise dans les diverses constitutions nationales.

Les gouvernements et les responsables sanitaires ont ainsi été confrontés à une problématique simple en apparence, mais dont la résolution n'était pas assurée : comment augmenter les capacités d'accueil des hôpitaux et des services de soins intensifs avec des infrastructures fixes et un personnel non démultipliable ? Si le problème des infrastructures a été résolu à grand renfort d'ingéniosité et de résilience, celui de la limitation du personnel s'est révélé beaucoup plus résistant. C'est ainsi que les horaires de travail ont été étendus et que des tâches ne correspondant pas au cahier des charges furent exigées. Parfois, les vacances planifiées furent annulées, les temps de formations effacés ou le personnel réaffecté. N'oublions pas non plus que les patients ont dû renoncer à certains droits, principalement celui de pouvoir être accompagnés et maintenir le contact avec son entourage.

Pendant une pandémie, les gouvernements démocratiques doivent trouver un équilibre. D'une part, ils doivent respecter, faire respecter et protéger les droits de l'homme tels que la liberté de réunion et l'égalité devant la loi. D'autre part, les droits de l'homme ont été restreints assez fortement afin de lutter contre la propagation de la maladie et la surcharge du système de santé. Par exemple, la liberté de circulation a été limitée dans de nombreux pays pour limiter les infections. Toutefois, si ces restrictions touchent la société dans son ensemble, c'est-à-dire tout le monde, les personnels de santé doivent supporter une charge plus importante. C'est leur travail (accru) qui permet de garantir de nombreux droits de l'homme pour tous. Ainsi, la politique, l'économie et la société placent des attentes et des exigences élevées sur le personnel de santé. On y voit un traitement inégal. Chacun doit se restreindre pour lutter contre la maladie, mais le personnel de santé doit en faire bien plus.

La question importante est donc : garantir le respect des droits de l'homme pour tous et du droit à l'égalité d'accès aux soins pour chaque être humain justifient les exigences élevées et extraordinaires imposées au personnel de santé ? La démocratie étant basée sur la majorité et l'urgence sanitaire frappant avec véhémence, cette voie fut privilégiée, privilégiée ou s'est imposée puisqu'étant la seule possible au vu des restrictions économiques dans le système de soins.

Ces exigences élevées et extraordinaires imposées à une petite frange de la société, à savoir le personnel soignant, se sont révélées nécessaires pour préserver les droits démocratiques de la majorité, c'est un fait. N'oublions pourtant pas que celles-ci n'ont été possibles que grâce à la solidarité, à la conscience professionnelle et à la résilience de ces professionnels. Au lendemain de l'urgence sanitaire, il faudra remettre en question la gestion même de la santé dans chaque pays : est-il normal d'en arriver à devoir exiger de ces êtres humains un don de soi au-delà du raisonnable ? Pourquoi a-t-on dû en exiger autant de ces hommes et femmes qui sont mis sous pression en permanence même hors crise ? Et surtout, la santé peut-elle continuer à être considérée comme n'importe quel bien de consommation ?

Dans cette crise, la rationalisation du système de santé pour atteindre une rentabilité a montré sa caducité manifeste. Pour tenir, pour assurer un accès égalitaire aux soins de santé, le personnel de santé a été énormément taxé. La gestion du système de santé doit être repensée pour que tant le quotidien que les crises sanitaires futures puissent être gérés décemment pour tous, dans un climat de confiance et le respect des droits de chacun.

2) Ageism and democracy in Switzerland: What we can learn from the Covid-19 pandemic

Marion Repetti[1]

In March 2020, facing the surge of Covid-19, the Swiss federal authorities enacted a "partial lockdown," enforcing social isolation to combat the pandemic and to avoid overcrowding in intensive care units in hospitals. They called on the population to shelter, that is to say, to stay at home as much as possible; this instruction was especially directed at "vulnerable" people, mostly at those aged 65 and over[2]. The protection of the latter age group was presented as a key priority in containing the spread of the disease. At that time, the Swiss national data showed that the average age of people who died from Covid-19 was in fact 81[3]. Yet, the increased risk of dying from Covid-19 with age has given legitimacy to these stricter measures towards older people. But, as this contribution will discuss, whilst they have been put at the core of pandemic policies, older people have also been—and still are—absent from the democratic debates regarding the social and economic consequences of these policies.

The social consequences of old people's social isolation

Although mortality by age group is similar internationally[4], the category "vulnerable people" in regard to Covid-19 covers

1 This contribution is an English translation with minor changes of an article previously published in the Revue d'Information Sociale. https://www.reiso.org/document/5879.

2 Federal Council. 6 March 2020. Coronavirus: mieux protéger les personnes vulnérables et évaluer l'impact économique de l'épidémie. https://www.admin.ch/gov/fr/accueil/documentation/communiques.msg-id-78381.html (Accessed 1 December, 2020).

3 Federal Office of Public Health. 2020. Covid-19 en Suisse. https://covid-19-schweiz.bagapps.ch/fr-1.html (Accessed 1 December, 2020).

4 Our World in Data. 2020. Case fatality rate of COVID-19 by age. https://ourworldindata.org/coronavirus#case-fatality-rate-of-covid-19-by-age (Accessed 1 December, 2020).

different groups across countries. The age at which this category starts to apply has been set at 70 in France[5] and the United Kingdom[6]. Other governments such as Germany[7] and the United States[8] have not selected a specific age in their policies. These variations suggest that the decision of the Swiss political authorities to set the threshold at which people are considered "vulnerable" at the age of 65 does not reflect purely statistical motivations. This age is in fact the one at which people can first access old-age insurance, and the one which Swiss state policies use to define the start of old age.

Although urgent measures were meant to protect people aged 65 and over, paradoxically, their voices have been largely absent from democratic debates about which policies to adopt as a response to the pandemic. The media have given a platform to political authorities, health experts and professionals, trade unions, and independent and small business representatives who are suffering the economic consequences of the partial lockdown. Whilst there are legitimate reasons for these groups to take part in the democratic debates on the consequences of the pandemic and the political responses to it, the invisibility of the people presented as the *raison d'être* of the measures is questionable. The social, emotional and psychological effects of sheltering have sometimes been mentioned in the media as particularly

5 Ministry of Solidarity and Health. 2020. https://solidarites-sante.gouv.fr/actualites/actualites-du-ministere/article/coronavirus-qui-sont-les-personnes-fragiles (Accessed 1 December, 2020).

6 Gov.UK. 2020. Coronavirus (COVID-19): Advice for vulnerable people. https://www.nidirect.gov.uk/articles/coronavirus-covid-19-advice-vulnerable-people (Accessed 1 December, 2020).

7 Bundeszentrale für gesundheitliche Aufklärung. 2020. Informationen zum neuartigen Coronavirus / COVID-19. https://www.infektionsschutz.de/coronavirus.html (Accessed 1 December, 2020).

8 Centers for Disease Control and Prevention. 2020. Coronavirus Disease 2019 (COVID-19). Older Adults. https://www.cdc.gov/coronavirus/2019-ncov/need-extra-precautions/older-adults.html (Accessed 1 December, 2020).

important for older people, but the legitimacy of a "stricter" confinement has only been rarely and belatedly discussed.

In reality, the strict social isolation of people aged 65 and over has had significant consequences for the social organisation and social cohesion of the country since the beginning of the pandemic. Firstly, it should be noted that older people's voluntary contributions as grandparents were quickly placed at the heart of the debate on whether or not to close schools. The authorities first wanted to keep schools open in order to prevent working parents from asking grandparents to look after their children. Some people then noted that the requirement to work outside of one's home already involved the need for grandparents to look after their grandchildren *before* the pandemic. Therefore, preventing older people from leaving their house was a problem for working parents, even if schools remained open. When the federal authorities subsequently closed schools, they enjoined companies to allow employees to work at home as much as possible, reinforcing the workload for parents—mostly for mothers. Parents (mostly mothers) had to both take care of their children, without the help of grandparents, and keep working for their employer from home. In this context, older people's role in the functioning of the Swiss economy has suddenly been revealed. Without them, the so-called "reconciliation" between work and family was compromised, requiring a fundamental revisiting of the daily organisation of most families.

Secondly, during the pandemic, anti-poverty charities lost the majority of their unpaid workers—i.e., older people—with dramatic consequences for precarious populations. Let us take the example of food banks in Switzerland, such as *Les*

Tables du Rhône in the canton of Valais[9]. Just like many other volunteer programmes, these are particularly dependent on the free social work provided by people aged 65 and over[10]. Without older people's contributions, their capacity is reduced, which in turn threatens to weaken social cohesion. And yet, in contrast to their role as grandparents—probably identified because it impacts on parents' abilities to maintain employment—older citizens' work to help poor and excluded groups in our society has received little political and media attention so far.

Heading towards the end of the year 2020, Switzerland is facing a second wave of Covid-19 and the authorities continue to call for older people to be more strictly confined than the rest of society. As for the absence of people aged 65 and over from charities, this has begun to be questioned[11]. Yet, older people are still scarcely consulted about Swiss pandemic policies. Paradoxically, although solidarity is now highly valued in the media, one of the most impacted groups (older people) remains ignored, in contrast to younger citizens whose contributions are regularly praised in the public debate. This discriminating political treatment of older people is not new in Switzerland—it is at the heart of the ageist social relations that structure our society, where each of us loses a share of power as we grow older. Although this loss of power takes place regardless of our social positioning, other power relations shape it, such

9 Associations Tables du Rhône. 2020. http://www.tablesdurhone.ch/ (Accessed 1 December, 2020).

10 Federal Statistical Office. 2018. Travail bénévole, part en % de chaque groupe de population accomplissant un travail bénévole institutionnalisé ou informel, selon le groupe d'âge, le type de ménage, le niveau de formation et le sexe. https://www.bfs.admin.ch/bfs/fr/home/statistiques/catalogues-banques-donnees/tableaux.assetdetail.5106554.html (Accessed 1 December, 2020).

11 Hartman, Dominique. 22 April 2020. Le travail bénévole s'essouffle. Le Courrier. https://lecourrier.ch/2020/04/23/le-travail-benevole-sessouffle/ (Accessed 10 December, 2020).

as gender, economic resources, ethnicity, and citizenship, among others. Thus, in the context of the Covid-19, older and poor people run a high risk of being invisible in public debates, especially if they are women.

The exclusion of older people from democratic debate

Political measures to combat Covid-19 reproduce age relations in Switzerland just like in other countries[12]. This situation highlights the difficulties that people encounter as they age in maintaining a legitimate place as actors in democratic debates. If the pandemic is to mark the organisation of our society in the long term, it seems essential to rethink this political treatment and to give older people a legitimate place as citizens. It is important to respect their democratic right and duty to participate in debates on the individual, social, political and economic consequences of measures which directly impact them. Their continued marginalisation has negative social consequences for society as a whole and positions older people as victims rather than as fully-fledged citizens, actors in a democratic society, and agents in their own lives.

12 Calasanti, Toni. 2020. Pervasive ageism in the response to the pandemic. ASA Footnotes. https://www.asanet.org/sites/default/files/attach/footnotes/may-june_2020_0.pdf;
Brooke, Joanne, and Jackson, Debra. 2020. Older people and COVID-19: Isolation, risk and ageism. Journal of Clinical Nursing, 29(13-14), 2044-2046;
Phillipson, Chris. 8 April 2020. Covid-19 and the crisis in residential and nursing home care. Ageing Issues. https://ageingissues.wordpress.com/2020/04/08/covid-19-and-the-crisis-in-residential-and-nursing-home-care/ (Accessed 1 December, 2020).

3) Risikogruppen – Über die Frage, wie gefährdet wir uns eigentlich fühlen

Christian Ewert

Auch wenn alle durch Covid-19 gefährdet werden, sind unterschiedliche Bevölkerungsgruppen unterschiedlichen Risiken ausgesetzt. Jüngere und gesunde Personen scheinen sich häufiger zu erholen; ältere und kranke Personen müssen eher mit Komplikationen rechnen.

Es überrascht daher nicht, dass im öffentlichen Diskurs von verschiedenen Risikogruppen gesprochen wird. Politiker und Politikerinnen, Angestellte der öffentlichen Verwaltung, Medien und andere Akteure unterteilen die Bevölkerung in weniger gefährdete und stärker gefährdete Gruppen. Im Winter 2020 stuft das schweizerische Bundesamt für Gesundheit vor allem Ältere und Schwangere als besonders gefährdet ein, ebenso Personen mit Vorerkrankungen wie etwa Bluthochdruck, Diabetes, chronischen Atemwegerkrankungen oder Krebs.[1]

Das Besondere an dieser Einteilung ist, dass sie zentralisiert und quasi von oben herab erfolgt. Es sind Experten und Expertinnen, Staatsangestellte und die Medien, welche Risikogruppen definieren. Eine weitere Besonderheit dieser Einteilung ist, dass sie objektiviert und rationalisiert wird. Die Einteilung der Bevölkerung in Gruppen erfolgt ja aufgrund wissenschaftlicher Kriterien. *Die Zahlen sprechen für sich,* so kann man es vielleicht paraphrasieren, *wenn man alt ist, dann ist man besonders gefährdet.* Man beachte, wie stark die Themen

1 Webseite des Bundesamtes für Gesundheit, https://www.bag.admin.ch/bag/de/home/krankheiten/ausbrueche-epidemien-pandemien/aktuelle-ausbrueche-epidemien/novel-cov/krankheit-symptome-behandlung-ursprung/besonders-gefaehrdete-menschen.html [Stand: 25. November 2020]

der (Lebens-)Gefahr und der Verwundbarkeit in dieser narrativen Gruppengestaltung enthalten sind.

Mit dieser objektivierten Einteilung beanspruchen Staat und Gesellschaft einmal mehr, wenigstens zum Teil über die Identität und Lebenserfahrung einzelner Menschen zu verfügen.[2] Es ist gerade nicht mehr jede Einzelperson, die bestimmt, wie sicher oder gefährdet sie ist, wie gesund oder krank. Es sind nun Experten und Expertinnen, Staatsangestellte und Medien, Erkenntnisse und Wissenschaft, die dies festlegen.

Ob und wie ein solcher Eingriff in die persönliche Lebensführung gerechtfertigt ist, muss an anderer Stelle beantwortet werden. Stattdessen möchte ich auf die Spannung hinweisen, welche entstehen kann, wenn objektivierte Gruppeneinteilung und individuelle Erfahrung der eigenen Lebenswirklichkeit auseinanderklaffen.

Gruppeneinteilungen, insbesondere solche, die aus einer Krisensituation heraus vorgenommen werden, sind weder wert- noch urteilsfrei. Im Gegenteil, Gruppenzugehörigkeit ist stets mit Erwartungshaltungen verbunden[3], was gerade für die Risikogruppen sichtbar wird. Wer alt ist, der/die ist besonders gefährdet, es wird daher von Politik und Gesellschaft erwartet, Schutzkonzepte zu erlassen und umzusetzen. Gleichzeitig wird von den Alten erwartet, sich selbst zu schützen, beispielsweise

---

2 Ein anderer Bereich, in dem das geschieht, ist die Armut. Das Bundesamt für Statistik erachtet Einzelpersonen dann als arm, wenn sie weniger als 2'293 CHF pro Monat zur Verfügung haben, bei einem Haushalt mit zwei Erwachsenen und zwei Kindern beträgt diese Grenze 3'968 CHF [Stand: 25. November 2020].

3 Für die Politikgestaltung wurden diese Erwartungshaltungen und Gruppenzugehörigkeiten aufgearbeitet von, zum Beispiel, Anne L. Schneider und Helen Ingram: Policy design for democracy, Lawrence: University Press of Kansas, 1997.

durch das Tragen von Masken, Desinfizieren von Händen oder Vermeiden von unnötigen sozialen Kontakten.

Die Zuteilung zur Risikogruppe einer Person, und die damit einhergehenden an sie gestellten Erwartungen, sind aber durchaus unabhängig von der individuellen Lebenserfahrung dieser Person[4]. Wer älter als 50 Jahre ist, kann sich sehr wohl gesund fühlen, kann sich als jung und stark erfahren. Wer eine Vorerkrankung hat, muss sich nicht als besonders gefährdet empfinden. Und konsequenterweise stellen solche Personen dann Erwartungen an sich und ihr Leben, welche von den gesellschaftlichen Erwartungen abweichen können.
Wer sich selbst als sicher erfährt, wird sich entsprechend verhalten, und zum Beispiel auf Maske tragen und Desinfizieren verzichten, oder unverändert soziale Kontakte suchen. Sollte diese Person «offiziell» zur Risikogruppe gehören, würde ihr tatsächliches Verhalten somit deutlich demjenigen Verhalten widersprechen, welches Staatsangestellte, Medien und andere Akteure von ihr erwarten.

Das Spannungsverhältnis existiert also zwischen den Erwartungen, welche «offiziell» von oben herab an die Gesellschaft gerichtet werden, und denen, die jeder Einzelne und jede Einzelne an sich und sein/ihr Leben stellt. Und dass es dieses Spannungsverhältnis überhaupt gibt, zeigt auf, wie begrenzt die Gestaltungsmacht des Staates eigentlich ist. Sicher, er kann Gesetze erlassen, Gefängnisse bauen und die gesamte Staatsmacht mobilisieren. Und doch bleibt sein Einfluss auf die individuelle Lebenserfahrung limitiert, selbst in der Extremsituation einer globalen Pandemie.

4 Jyotirmaya Tripathy (2017): The development language: BPL category and the poverty discourse in contemporary India, Social Semiotics, 28(3), 396-411.

4) Schulschliessungen und demokratische Sozialisierung der Kinder

Franziska Hedinger

Als sich im Frühling 2020 Covid-19 immer mehr ausbreitete, beschlossen viele Regierungen zur Eindämmung der Pandemie die Schulen zu schliessen. Als erstes demokratisches Land stellte Italien bereits Ende Februar den normalen Schulbetrieb ein. Mitte März hatten praktisch alle westlichen Demokratien den Präsenzunterricht an den Schulen verboten. Auf dem Höhepunkt der Schulschliessungen im Frühling blieben weltweit fast 90 Prozent der Schülerinnen und Schüler dem regulären Schulbetrieb fern. In der Schweiz dauerte der verhängte Fernunterricht gut zwei Monate, in Italien sahen die Schülerinnen und Schüler ihre Schulen über ein halbes Jahr nicht mehr von innen.[1]

Mit der Bildung als wichtiges Gut, welches Staaten ihren Kindern zur Verfügung stellen sollen, kamen Bedenken gegenüber den Schulschliessungen auf. Selbsterklärend war die Gesellschaft skeptisch, ob die Schülerinnen und Schüler durch das Home-Schooling weniger lernen und wichtigen Stoff verpassen würden. Zudem befürchtete man, dass sich die Schere zwischen guten und schlechten Lernenden weiter öffnen würde. Weiter hatte man Bedenken, dass sich die Startchancen fürs spätere (Berufs-)Leben von sozioökonomisch benachteiligten Kinder durch den Fernunterricht verschlechtern könnten. Ebenso machte man sich Sorgen, was für einen psychologischen Effekt längere Schulschliessungen auf die jungen Menschen haben könnte.[2]

---

1 UNESCO. 2020. Gobal Monitoring of school closures caused by COVID-19. https://en.unesco.org/covid19/educationresponse

2 Huber, Stephan G., Günther, Paula Sophie, Schneider, Nadine, Helm, Christoph, Schwander, Marius, Schneider, Julia A., Pruitt, Jane. 2020. COVID-19 und aktuelle

Denkt man an die Aufgabe der Schule, dann ist klar, dass die Heranwachsenden dort «etwas» lernen sollen. Jedoch hat die Schule auch eine Funktion, welche im Zusammenhang mit den Schulschliessungen weniger besprochen wurde. Neben der «Lehrfunktion» erfüllt die Schule nämlich auch eine soziokulturelle Integrationsfunktion. Unter dieser Funktion versteht die Bildungswissenschaft die Schulen als «Instrumente der gesellschaftlichen Integration». Denn die Schulen geben Normen, Werte und Weltsichten wieder, welche in einer Gesellschaft vorherrschen. Die Schulen erschaffen in Demokratien somit ein soziales Zusammengehörigkeitsgefühl und eine kulturelle Identifikation. Schulen tragen also zum inneren Zusammenhalt einer demokratischen Gesellschaft bei und schaffen Vertrauen in die demokratischen Werte.[3] Diese sind für die Existenzfähigkeit von Demokratien bedeutend. Die politikwissenschaftliche Forschung zeigt, dass für eine funktionierende Demokratie die demokratische Einstellung der Gesellschaft eine nicht zu unterschätzende Rolle spielt.[4]

Ein massgebliches Prinzip der Demokratie ist, dass politische und soziale Differenzen durch öffentliche Diskussionen und durch Meinungsaustausch ausgehandelt werden. Gemeinschaftlich und über soziale Schichten hinweg werden so Lösungen für gesamtgesellschaftliche Probleme gesucht. Im Zusammenhang mit der soziokulturellen Integrationsfunktion können Schulen daher «als erste Kreise der demokratischen Gesellschaft»[5] betrachtet werden. Der Pausenhof und die

---

Herausforderungen in Schule und Bildung: erste Befunde des Schul-Barometers in Deutschland, Österreich und der Schweiz. Münster: Waxmann.

3 Fend, Helmut. 2008. Neue Theorie der Schule: Einführung in das Verstehen von Bildungssystemen. 2. Aufl. Wiesbaden: Verlag für Sozialwissenschaften. S. 47-50.

4 Almond, Gabriel Abraham, und Sidney Verba. 1963. The Civic Culture: Political Attitudes and Democracy in Five Nations. Princeton: Sage.

5 Oelkers, Jürgen. 2000. „Demokratie und Bildung: Über die Zukunft eines Problems". Zeitschrift für Pädagogik 46(3): S. 333–47. S. 503.

Klassenräume stellen eine Art kleine Gemeinschaft dar, denn durch die Schulpflicht vereint die Schule den gesamten Nachwuchs einer Gesellschaft an einem einzigen Ort.[6] Die Schulen, in denen Schülerinnen und Schüler täglich einander begegnen, sind somit kleinräumige Gesellschaften in denen die Jugendlichen erste Erfahrungen im Austausch mit anderen sammeln. Diese privaten Auseinandersetzungen stellen für die Jugendlichen ein Übungsfeld dar, in dem sie die Fähigkeit des fairen Aushandelns von demokratischen Regeln und Normen lernen. Mit Altersgleichen können sie in dieser kleinen Gemeinschaft lernen «auf sich aufmerksam zu machen, gehört zu werden, akzeptiert zu werden, sich durchzusetzen, Kompromisse zu schliessen»[7] sowie weitere zivile Kompetenzen erwerben. Diese «demokratischen» Erfahrungen tragen die Jugendlichen nach ihren Schuljahren in die Gesellschaft hinaus. Bleiben Schulen über längere Zeit geschlossen, fehlt einer ganzen Generation für diese Dauer dieser Erfahrungsraum, welcher für die demokratische Sozialisierung wichtig ist.

Die in diesem Frühjahr vollzogenen Schulschliessungen werden aufgrund ihrer «kurzen» Dauer im Vergleich zur obligatorischen Schulzeit keine undemokratischen Jugendlichen aus den Schulen entlassen. Dennoch lohnt es sich, auch über diese Problematik zu reflektieren und diskutieren.

---

6 Hollenstein, Oliver, Tobias Leonhard, und Christine Schlickum. 2019. „Schule aus erziehungswissenschaftlicher Perspektive". In Handbuch Schulpädagogik, Hrsg. Marius Harring, Carsten Rohlfs, und Michaela Gläser-Zikuda. Münster: Waxmann, S. 54–63. S. 59.

7 Fend, Helmut. 2008. S. 73.

5) Lockdown, Maskenpflicht und Co. – Wie man aussergewöhnliche Massnahmen begründen kann

Christian Ewert

Im Kampf gegen das Coronavirus werden unterschiedliche Massnahmen ergriffen. Manche davon, wie das Einrichten von Möglichkeiten, sich beim Betreten eines Geschäftes die Hände zu desinfizieren, schränken den Alltag wenig ein. Andere Massnahmen sind dagegen sehr invasiv, tangieren Menschen- und Bürgerrechte und sind vor allem für eine freiheitlich-demokratische Gesellschaft sehr aussergewöhnlich.
Dazu gehören sicherlich Maskenpflicht, Restriktionen für Gastrobetriebe oder ein Lockdown. Je einschränkender und umfangreicher eine Massnahme, desto überzeugender muss sie auch begründet, erklärt und legitimiert werden.

Im demokratischen Rechtsstaat ist eine solche Legitimierung einerseits immer eine juristische Frage. Zum Beispiel kann man fragen, ob der Bundesrat überhaupt die Kompetenzen besitzt, um einen landesweiten Lockdown mit all seinen wirtschaftlichen und gesellschaftlichen Konsequenzen anzuordnen. Es braucht also auf jeden Fall eine formelle, rechtliche Legitimierung.

Andererseits findet Politik in Ländern wie der Schweiz auch immer vor einem Publikum, also den Bürgern und Bürgerinnen, statt. Gerade strenge Massnahmen müssen von allen mitgetragen werden, damit sie wirken. Und für dieses *Mittragen* ist es eben nötig, dass alle von der Notwendigkeit, Angemessenheit und Erwünschtheit der (aussergewöhnlichen) Massnahmen überzeugt sind.[1] In anderen Worten, diese

1 Feldman, Y. (2011), Five models of regulatory compliance motivation: empirical findings and normative implications, in David Levi-Faur, ed., Handbook on the

Massnahmen müssen nicht nur «objektiv» durch das Gesetz gestützt sein, sondern auch «subjektiv» von Bürgern und Bürgerinnen als angemessen und wünschenswert beurteilt werden.[2] Ausserdem müssen sich diejenigen, welche heute solche Massnahmen erlassen (oder dies gerade nicht tun), in einiger Zeit demokratischen Wahlen stellen. Es gibt also noch einen Grund mehr, Massnahmen zu begründen und legitimieren.

Wie kann man nun aber Massnahmen wie einen Lockdown oder eine allgemeine Maskenpflicht legitimieren? Die Forschung zur politischen Kommunikation hat mehrere rhetorische Mittel identifiziert, die von politischen Akteuren verwendet und kombiniert werden können; ich möchte diese Mittel im Folgenden kurz vorstellen.[3]

Erstes Mittel: Auf Emotionen wie Angst verweisen
Emotionen, insbesondere die Angst, werden oft in der politischen Kommunikation referenziert. Zum Beispiel kann eine Verschärfung der Einbürgerungsrechts rhetorisch durch einen Verweis auf die Angst vor Überfremdung begründet werden. Im Falle von Covid-19 scheint die Verwendung der Angst allerdings ein zweischneidiges Schwert zu sein. Einerseits breitet sich die Krankheit rasant aus und ist vor allem für bestimmte Bevölkerungsgruppen lebensgefährlich. Andererseits streiten viele Akteure die Gefährlichkeit ab oder spielen sie herunter. Ausserdem verläuft eine Ansteckung für die meisten jungen und gesunden Menschen eher harmlos. In anderen Worten, viele Personen scheinen Covid-19 nicht

---

Politics of Regulation, Cheltenham: Edward Elgar, pp. 335-346.

2 Suchman, M. C. (1995), Managing Legitimacy: Strategic and Institutional Approaches, The Academy of Management Review, 20(3), 571-610.

3 Reyes, A. (2011), Strategies of Legitimization in Political Discourse: From Words to Actions, Discourse & Society, 22(6), 781-807.

sonderlich zu fürchten, weswegen sie Angstverweise als rhetorische Mittel nur bedingt überzeugen.

Zweites Mittel: Eine hypothetische Zukunft konstruieren
Politische Akteure können eine hypothetische Zukunft erzeugen, was meistens konditional, also durch eine *Wenn-Dann* Konstruktion, erfolgt. Die hypothetische Zukunft kann positiv oder negativ konnotiert sein. Zum Beispiel: «Wenn die Masken nicht getragen werden, dann wird sich die Krankheit weiter ausbreiten». Aber auch: «Wenn wir die Infektionen jetzt eindämmen können, dann braucht es keinen zweiten Lockdown». Bei der Konstruktion ist es wichtig, dass die hypothetische Zukunft glaubwürdig ist, und entweder bedrohlich (negative Zukunft) oder wünschenswert (positive Zukunft) erscheint. Man darf vermuten, dass dieses rhetorische Mittel dann wirksam wird, wenn die Menschen bereits Erfahrung mit der Krankheit sammeln konnten. Zur Illustration: Je glaubwürdiger und je bedrohlicher ein neuer Lockdown wirkt (weil vorherige Lockdowns noch gut in Erinnerung sind), desto eher überzeugt es, wenn er «angedroht» wird.

Drittes Mittel: Auf die Rationalität des Entscheidungsprozesses hinweisen
Anstatt eine Entscheidung oder Massnahme zu begründen, können politische Akteure auch auf den Prozess hinweisen, in dem die Entscheidung oder Massnahme entwickelt oder gefunden wurde. In der Schweiz gibt es zum Beispiel das Vernehmlassungsverfahren, in dem wichtige Akteure ihre Positionen zu einer Gesetzesänderung bekunden können. Auch der Schweizer Bundesrat hat bei neuen Massnahmen wiederholt darauf hingewiesen, dass etwa Kantone vorgängig angehört wurden.

Viertes Mittel: Experten und Expertinnen involvieren
Experten oder Expertinnen wie etwa Medizinerinnen oder hohe Beamte werden oft «instrumentalisiert», um neue Massnahmen zu begründen. Zum Beispiel übergibt der Bundesrat in Pressekonferenzen oft das Wort an leitende Staatsangestellte, damit diese Detailfragen beantworten und so Vertrauen erwecken können. Dieses rhetorische Mittel wird aber nur dann die gewünschte Wirkung entfalten, wenn die Autorität der Experten und Expertinnen gegeben ist, diese Personen also als vertrauenswürdig akzeptiert werden. Daher können ihre Stimmen in Krisensituationen besonders wichtig werden, während gleichzeitig ihre Glaubwürdigkeit im öffentlichen Diskurs diskreditiert wird. Als tragisches Beispiel kann der US-Amerikaner Dr. Anthony S. Fauci gelten, der von manchen Menschen als kompetent und vertrauenswürdig angesehen wird, aber gleichzeitig auch von Donald Trumps Wahlkampfteam diffamiert wurde.[4]

Fünftes Mittel: An das Gemeinwohl appellieren
Man kann nicht nur Emotionen ansprechen, sondern auch Werte, wie etwa Patriotismus oder Nächstenliebe. Sehr häufig werden Entscheidungen oder Massnahmen rhetorisch durch altruistische Werte begründet. Das Argument ist dann, dass nicht nur einzelne von einer Massnahme profitieren, sondern dass die Allgemeinheit etwas davon hat. Die Schwierigkeit ist natürlich, dass die Interessen der Allgemeinheit nicht eindeutig sind; dies wird insbesondere während der aktuellen Pandemie deutlich. Ein neuer Lockdown hätte zwar positive Folgen auf die öffentliche Gesundheit, würde aber der Wirtschaft massiv schaden. Entsprechend wird zwischen

4 Siehe BBC News: https://www.bbc.com/news/world-us-canada-53392817 [Stand: 29. November 2020] aber auch Forbes: https://www.forbes.com/sites/brucelee/2020/05/10/anthony-fauci-is-facing-online-attacks-and-covid-19-coronavirus-conspiracy-theories/ [Stand: 29. November 2020]

der öffentlichen Gesundheit und einer funktionierenden Wirtschaft abgewogen. Man darf daher vermuten, dass Appelle an das Gemeinwohl momentan weniger wirken könnten.

Man kann also festhalten, dass vor allem die aussergewöhnlichen Massnahmen gegen Covid-19 besonders gute Begründungen brauchen. Neben den formal-rechtlichen Grundlagen braucht es aber auch die Unterstützung und Anerkennung von Bürgern und Bürgerinnen. Die Politik wird daher versuchen, die Massnahmen durch den Einsatz der genannten rhetorischen Mittel zu begründen. Der vorliegende Beitrag konnte nun hoffentlich andeuten, dass diese rhetorischen Mittel Bedingungen unterliegen und gerade während einer Pandemie nicht jeden überzeugen werden. Eine aussergewöhnliche Lage erfordert deshalb in der Tat nicht nur aussergewöhnliche Massnahmen, sondern auch eine aussergewöhnliche Rhetorik.

6) (Un)masking the Demos: How Covid-19 Containment Policies Conceal State Surveillance

Hans Asenbaum

The Covid-19 pandemic has introduced us to someone new, an acquaintance with whom we have established an intimate relationship within a very short time—the face mask. Masks have become a device found in every household, an object of everyday use. Masks also take a prominent role in democratic engagement. They function as a symbol promoting pandemic containment policies when they are worn by politicians giving speeches in election campaigns or when they are worn in parliamentary debates. They become an object of contention when unmasked protesters challenge Covid-19 policies in street rallies. Masks, finally, have become a necessity for most people who gather publicly to promote or contest various, health-unrelated causes[1].

While the sight of a protesting masked crowd might appear uncommon, masks have actually played a central role in public demonstrations for a long time. Recent examples include the Guy Fawkes mask worn by Anonymous and the Occupy movement, the colourful balaclavas of Pussy Riot, the face coverings of the Mexican Zapatistas, the plastic gorilla masks of the feminist art collective Guerilla Girls, the black balaclavas of the anarchist Black Bloc, and the hoods of the Black Lives Matter movement. Masking and disguise also play a crucial role in the annual pride parades, which celebrate sexual diversity. The history of political masking can even be traced back to the medieval carnival, in which regular people

1 Parry, L., Asenbaum, H. and Ercan, S. (2020) 'Democracy in Flux: a Systemic View on the Impact of COVID-19', Transforming Government: People, Process and Policies, 0(0), pp. 1–11. doi: 10.1108/TG-09-2020-0269.

dressed as kings, queens, and popes to mock those in power and challenge social hierarchies. In all of these examples, the mask fulfils a double role. It hides the identity of the person who wears it. But at the same time, it also creates a new identity. In the context of political protest, the mask creates a political identity that stands for a certain cause[2].

State power has shown itself to be not amused by such frivolous contestations. It neither appreciates its subjects attempts to escape the state's watchful eye, nor the contentious identities produced by the mask's anonymity. The medieval torture and even execution of those who took the mockery too far is mirrored in today's laws that sanction masking in public protest. Canada, for example, punishes wearing masks at unlawful protests with up to ten years in prison. Anti-masking laws were originally installed in the USA to curtail the activities of the Ku Klux Klan. Today, however, they are challenged for stifling free speech when they prohibit protesters of the freedom of information movement from wearing the white, grinning Guy Fawkes mask. The ambiguity of anti-masking laws is further increased when they are directed against the public veiling wearing of Muslim women, which aims to protect women's autonomy but at the same time functions to amplify racist resentments[3].

Beyond this ambiguity, anti-masking laws need to be read in the context of a new emerging surveillance state that tracks and traces its citizens' movements and collects unimaginable

---

2 Asenbaum, H. (2018) 'Anonymity and Democracy: Absence as Presence in the Public Sphere', American Political Science Review, 112(3), pp. 459–472. doi: https://doi.org/10.1017/S0003055418000163.

3 Ruiz, P. (2013) 'Revealing Power: Masked Protest and the Blank Figure', Cultural Politics, 9(3), pp. 263–279. doi: 10.1215/17432197-2346973.; Spiegel, J. (2015) 'Masked Protest in the Age of Austerity: State Violence, Anonymous Bodies, and Resistance "In the Red"', Critical Inquiry, 41(4), pp. 786–810.

amounts of personal data online. Public space today is marked by the presence of surveillance cameras operating with ever more sophisticated face recognition software. It is the state's interest to access the individual, to identify and control its subjects[4]. The state assumes the role of Big Brother, who is attempting to unmask the demos.

With the onset of the Covid-19 pandemic, however, things have taken an unexpected turn. State governments now call for public masking. Protest is only possible with face coverings. The state is masking the demos. What an irony! Similarly, from the view of protesters the mask has changed its meaning. From signalling resistance to state intrusion into privacy, from making a statement for free speech, the face mask in public protest has become a symbol for compliance with the state and its pandemic containment policies. Masking in itself is not an act of carnivalesque protest anymore. Instead of a playful contestation, the mask now articulates a consensual identity. It signifies an agreement between the state and protestors to protect public health.

This new consensus does not, however, fundamentally alter the roles and interests of the two parties. Protesters might embrace masking more readily, because it is in accordance with their original intent to be shielded from state intrusion. The state, in contrast, still seeks to identify, document, and control its subjects. What is crucial, however, is that while the state concedes to a temporary masking of the demos in public protest, it extends its grip on personal identity by establishing digital tracking tools. These contact tracing apps record individual locations via GPS and alert users to heightened

4 de Lagasnerie, G. (2017) The Art of Revolution: Snowden, Assange, Manning. Stanford: Stanford University Press.

risks of contamination. Of course, these apps are designed specifically to deal with the Covid-19 pandemic. But they might contribute to a gradual change in the public attitude toward such surveillance tools. If preventing infection through digital tracking is welcome, why would preventing crime not be? Before the pandemic, it would have been absolutely unthinkable for governments in established democracies to openly develop and advertise digital technologies to track individuals and for the public to embrace these technologies and use them voluntarily. The state's new acceptance of masked protesting, then, stands in contrast with its continuous effort to access the private individual.

– B –

Politische Implikationen
Les implications politiques
Implicazioni politiche
Political implications

Politische Implikationen

Wie kann man den Herausforderungen der Pandemie politisch begegnen? Und wie reagieren demokratische Staaten und politische Akteure auf diese Ausnahmesituation? Welche Akteure profitieren, welche gewinnen an Macht oder Glaubwürdigkeit? Wie verändern sich demokratische Prozesse?

Les implications politiques

Comment relever les défis créés par la pandémie sur le plan politique ? Et comment les États démocratiques et les acteurs politiques réagissent-ils à cette situation exceptionnelle ? Quels sont les acteurs qui en bénéficient, qui gagnent en pouvoir ou en crédibilité ? Comment les processus démocratiques changent-ils ?

Implicazioni politiche

Come si possono affrontare le sfide della pandemia sul piano politico? Come reagiscono gli Stati democratici e gli attori politici di fronte a questa situazione straordinaria? Quali attori ne beneficiano, quali guadagnano potere o credibilità? Come cambiano i processi democratici?

Political implications

How can the challenges of the pandemic be met politically? And how do democratic states and political actors react to this exceptional situation? Which actors benefit, which gain power or credibility? How do democratic processes change?

7) How to "solve" a global pandemic?

Christian Ewert

At first glance, the emergence and spread of Covid-19 seems to be a problem of public health. It is a disease, after all, that has infected and killed many people and eventually turned into the global pandemic it is today. This problem calls for governmental intervention, for regulations, orders, rules and the like. Is it not the job of governments, we might ask, to deal with problems of public concern?

Let us take a step back, though, and reflect a bit more on what *kind* of a problem Covid-19 might be. Indeed, the literature on public policy and policy design has long emphasized the relevance of problem definitions[1]. On the one hand, we have seen many people who *do not* define Covid-19 as a problem at all. Donald Trump, for example, has repeatedly downplayed the severeness of this disease. He compared Covid-19 to the flu in a tweet on 6 October 2020. And while being infected himself, he went for a short trip to wave to his supporters in Bethesda, Maryland, two days earlier. Apart from him, people who refuse to wear masks are a common sight in many countries.

On the other hand, we also find many different problem definitions (and hence proposals for solutions too) that acknowledge the disease's danger. While much of Europe was locked down during the first wave, Sweden and the United Kingdom found their very own peculiar responses to the pandemic. Likewise, when the numbers of infected rose significantly and thus indicated a second wave, many

1 For example: Burstein, P. and Bricher, M. (1997), Problem Definition and Public Policy: Congressional Committees Confront Work, Family, and Gender, 1945-1990, Social Forces, 75(4), 135-169.

European countries implemented stern restrictions. Yet Switzerland, with some of the highest rates in comparison, only applied limited measures at the time of this writing.

But apart from the contestations concerning its threat, the pandemic shows some traits that make it a particularly "wicked" problem[2] to solve. With this I don't mean the difficulty to find a cure or a vaccine. Instead, I refer to the *political* difficulty to find an effective response to the pandemic.

What, then, makes a problem "wicked," that is to say, particularly difficult to deal with? Due to the limitations in space, I will discuss only two characteristics of such problems.

For one, a wicked problem never comes alone. It is rather always symptomatic of other closely associated problems. Covid-19 is an infectious disease, and while many that have become infected do not need intensive medical treatment, some do. Given the spread of the disease, it is thus closely associated with the public health system's limited capacities. This was apparent the most during the first wave, when many hospitals were overwhelmed by the sheer number of patients who needed care. Furthermore, the pandemic is also associated with the economic situation. Markets need to be running to function and any lockdown—which would help to contain the disease—creates severe financial disruptions. Even more so, and to name a last example, many states are too "depleted"[3] financially to maintain a wide and robust social net that would carry their populations through difficult times.

2 Rittel, H. W. J. and Webber, M. M. (1984), Planning Problems are Wicked Problems, in Nigel Cross , ed., Developments in Design Methodology, Chichester: John Wiley & Sons, pp. 135-144.

3 Lodge, M. (2013), Crisis, Resources and the State: Executive Politics in the Age of the Depleted State, Political Studies Review, 11, 378-390.

As a consequence, if one attempts to solve a wicked problem, one faces not one problem but many at once. And every attempt to solve a wicked problem affects other issue areas as well, causes "ripples" and "cascades" with unforeseen implications.

A second characteristic of wicked problems is that our ability to learn to solve them is very limited. Compare the game of chess in contrast, which is typically called a "tame" problem. After we have played a game of chess, we can put all pieces back to their starting positions and start playing anew. By playing chess over and over again, we become better, we learn. We understand how to solve chess. This is not possible with the pandemic. The decision to go into lockdown cannot be taken back or undone. We can neither return to the starting position because every intervention (and nonintervention) has an impact and changes the situation.

In other words, we cannot learn how to solve a wicked problem because every solution we try modifies its very nature. Every time we face a wicked problem it has already become a new problem. For example, although we can in hindsight, at least in theory, determine the effects of a first lockdown, we can never fully foresee the impact a second one might have.

We can thus say that wicked problems are, in general, very *deep* because they are connected to many other social, economic, and political issues. Wicked problems are also quite *volatile* since they change whenever we interact with them.

For sure, governments can "meddle" with the pandemic. Perhaps they manage to reduce the number of infections or perhaps they fail to do so. But with every measure that is implemented, whether it makes the situation better or worse, new problems will be created for society, the economy, and politics. In the end, a measure might do more damage than it does good. And governments cannot fully anticipate the implications of their measures because of the problem's changing nature. Given that Covid-19 is a wicked problem, there is no straightforward solution, and maybe the best we can do is indeed to "meddle through."

8) Come gestiremo le crisi che verranno? Uno sguardo a soluzioni più democratiche

Chiara Valsangiacomo

Marzo 2020 è stato un mese di decisioni storiche ed impensabili per la democrazia Svizzera. Fra il 15 ed il 18 marzo, la sessione in corso dell'assemblea federale veniva sospesa, il consiglio federale proclamava la 'situazione straordinaria' su tutto il territorio svizzero, e la votazione popolare di maggio veniva rinviata a data indefinita. Questo stato emergenziale si è poi concluso il 19 giugno, e da allora vige una cosiddetta 'situazione particolare'.[1] Intanto, i cittadini svizzeri sono tornati ad esprimersi durante le votazioni popolari di settembre e novembre. Il parlamento si è riunito prima durante una sessione straordinaria a maggio, poi per le sessioni ordinarie estive ed autunnali, mentre in questi giorni è indaffarato con l'ultima sessione dell'anno. Ai cantoni invece è tornata ampia competenza nel disporre vari provvedimenti per far fronte alla pandemia, seppur in stretta collaborazione con la confederazione. Ad oggi, mentre impennano i nuovi casi, il consiglio federale non sembra intenzionato a riattivare nuovamente la situazione straordinaria.[2]

Da un punto di vista istituzionale, dunque, il sistema democratico svizzero sembra tornare verso una certa normalità pre-crisi, nonostante la situazione resti complessa. Per ogni sostenitore della democrazia, questo deve essere un

1 Confederazione Svizzera (2020): Uscita dalla situazione straordinaria – trasposizione dell'ordinanza 2 COVID-19 nel diritto ordinario. Scheda informativa, 19 giugno 2020. https://www.newsd.admin.ch/newsd/message/attachments/61796.pdf

2 Corriere del Ticino (2020): Una nuova situazione straordinaria? Solo come ultima spiaggia. Corriere del Ticino, 17 ottobre 2020. https://www.cdt.ch/svizzera/una-nuova-situazione-straordinaria-solo-come-ultima-spiaggia-MF3315086?_sid=JEEzfknS

risultato incoraggiante e per niente scontato, specialmente in ottica comparativa.[3] Ad esempio, in Italia lo stato di emergenza per fare fronte alla crisi vige senza interruzioni dal 31 gennaio 2020, e anche Francia e Spagna hanno dichiarato per la seconda volta lo stato di emergenza nazionale a partire, rispettivamente, dal 17 e 25 ottobre 2020.[4] In questi tre casi, proprio come in Svizzera, le azioni dei rispettivi governi sono state certamente prese in conformità delle leggi[5] e nel rispetto di principi democratici, come la temporaneità delle misure adottate, la proporzionalità delle decisioni e la trasparenza delle procedure.[6] Eppure, non è mancata la pioggia di critiche riguardo all'accentramento del potere nelle mani degli organi esecutivi (i governi) e alla marginalizzazione degli organi legislativi (i parlamenti). In molti, giornalisti e studiosi, hanno espresso scetticismo e talvolta disaccordo con le modalità di gestione della crisi.

Questo articolo pone le seguenti domande di natura teorica: quanto è sostenibile, per una democrazia avanzata del ventunesimo secolo e per i suoi cittadini e cittadine, operare sotto un simile regime eccezionale? Se nel medio e lungo termine tale regime risulta indesiderabile, quali alternative

3 Bruno Kaufmann (2020): Come il coronavirus ha colpito la democrazia in tutto il mondo. Swissinfo, 31 marzo 2020. https://www.swissinfo.ch/ita/-no-time-to-die-_come-il-coronavirus-ha-colpito-la-democrazia-in-tutto-il-mondo/45653628

4 Governo italiano (2020): Coronavirus, le misure adottate dal Governo. http://www.governo.it/it/coronavirus-misure-del-governo; Swissinfo (2020): Coronavirus: Francia proroga stato d'emergenza fino al 16 febbraio. Swissinfo, 21 ottobre 2020. https://www.swissinfo.ch/ita/tutte-le-notizie-in-breve/coronavirus--francia-proroga-stato-d-emergenza-fino-al-16-febbraio/46111274; Swissinfo (2020): Coronavirus: la Spagna dichiara lo stato d'emergenza. Swissinfo, 25 ottobre 2020. https://www.swissinfo.ch/ita/tutte-le-notizie-in-breve/coronavirus--la-spagna-dichiara-lo-stato-d-emergenza/46119420

5 Legge federale del 28 settembre 2012 sulla lotta contro le malattie trasmissibili dell'essere umano (LEp, RS 818.101, Art. 6, Art. 7). https://www.admin.ch/opc/it/classified-compilation/20071012/index.html#a7; Costituzione Federale della Confederazione Svizzera del 18 aprile 1999 (BV, RS 101, Art. 36). https://www.admin.ch/opc/it/classified-compilation/19995395/index.html#a36

6 Università di Siena (2020): 'La democrazia alla prova del coronavirus' con Tania Groppi. Youtube, 23 aprile 2020. https://www.youtube.com/watch?v=D2L-AANG-To

si presentano per gestire le crisi nazionali in modo ancora più democratico e legittimo? Questo breve articolo non può di certo dare una risposta definitiva e universale a queste domande, ciononostante si limita a tematizzare il problema ed offrire una panoramica delle possibili soluzioni.

Le crisi – come quella attuale del coronavirus, ma prima di lei quelle finanziarie e del terrorismo – sono eventi critici, tecnici e complessi. Le crisi sono critiche nel senso che dirompono improvvisamente, causando un'acuta minaccia per la sicurezza e la stabilità di una società, e quindi richiedono una risposta altrettanto rapida per evitare un alteramento totale e irreversibile degli equilibri esistenti. Richiedono risposte tecniche e competenti perché riguardano ed elevano a priorità ambiti specifici della società, come la salute pubblica. Sono complesse perché le scelte prese durante la crisi possono avere ripercussioni più o meno gravi e durature su altri ambiti importanti della società. Per affrontare una crisi, sembra allora spontaneo scegliere una catena di comando verticale, semplice e con ruoli e responsabilità ben delineati. Questo consente una gestione della crisi rapida, efficiente, chiara e competente. Non stupisce dunque che i principali attori coinvolti nell'attuale crisi e, di riflesso, nel discorso pubblico siano, da un lato, esperti di medicina e della salute pubblica e, dall'altro lato, i pochi membri dei vari organi esecutivi federali e cantonali.

Alla luce di tutto questo, resta da giustificare il perché della marginalizzazione dei cittadini e delle cittadine come pure del parlamento – una tendenza che, come detto, è stata breve e moderata in Svizzera rispetto ad altri paesi. Non è infatti evidente il motivo, o i motivi, per cui cittadini e parlamento non possano continuare ad adempiere ai loro essenziali ruoli di sorveglianza e legiferazione anche in tempi emergenziali. Dal punto di vista consequenziale (per cui il fine giustifica i mezzi), bisogna chiedersi se è vero che concedere all'organo esecutivo pieni poteri, fra cui la facoltà di emanare leggi, sia l'unica soluzione efficace in una situazione straordinaria. Se ciò risultasse vero, bisognerebbe mettere in discussione la democrazia stessa come metodo di governo e soprattutto spiegare perché una simile logica strumentale non si applichi in tempi ordinari. Se invece ciò fosse almeno in parte falso, concedere un ruolo più rilevante a parlamenti e cittadini non pregiudicherebbe automaticamente il risultato finale, ossia un soddisfacente superamento della crisi. Dal punto di vista deontologico (per cui certi principi e procedure decisionali sono intrinsecamente superiori e preferibili ad altre), l'accentramento di potere nelle mani degli organi esecutivi rappresenta, per definizione, un problema per la democrazia. Già da tempo molti paesi democratici sembrano adottare un approccio pragmatico, una soluzione di mezzo fra questi due punti di vista, per cui si desidera una gestione efficiente delle emergenze che al contempo non comprometta totalmente i valori e le istituzioni democratiche. Non è quindi assurdo riflettere e proporre misure per rendere ancor più democratica la gestione delle crisi – se non di quella presente, almeno di quelle future.

Il parlamento è l'organo democratico per eccellenza in quanto sede di rappresentanza del popolo. Fra le varie funzioni essenziali del parlamento, vi è la sorveglianza delle attività del governo. È strano pensare, allora, che la situazione straordinaria in Svizzera sia stata decisa e annunciata dal consiglio federale. Se da un lato bisogna riconoscere che quest'ultimo è responsabile del coordinamento e della comunicazione con i cantoni, e quindi è un attore fondamentale nel processo che porta a decretare uno stato straordinario e al rafforzamento dello stato centrale, la decisione ufficiale riguardo all'inizio e la fine dello stato di necessità dovrebbe comunque spettare al parlamento.[7] Questo è un elemento che potrebbe essere corretto in futuro, a livello sia federale che cantonale. Inoltre, il coinvolgimento del parlamento potrebbe e dovrebbe essere più ampio, specialmente durante un'emergenza di natura non bellica. In forma fisica o virtuale, i membri del parlamento e le commissioni parlamentari dovrebbero potersi riunire per deliberare e decidere almeno a proposito delle questioni più urgenti, e venire coinvolti nelle scelte del consiglio federale in tempi reali. A livello mediatico, il ruolo del parlamento potrebbe essere più presente e visibile agli occhi del cittadino, affinché quest'ultimo non dubiti che i suoi interessi siano stati illegittimamente estromessi.

Oltre a questo, in futuro si potrebbero considerare soluzioni che coinvolgano più direttamente i cittadini e le cittadine. Una pratica interessante è la creazione di un cosiddetto concilio cittadino d'emergenza, un gruppo di cittadini estratti a sorte per partecipare ad un processo deliberativo riguardante la gestione dell'emergenza.[8] Quest'idea è strettamente collegata al fenomeno dei *mini publics* e rappresenta una variante molto più raffinata ed informativa di un normale sondaggio: con un tale processo si approssimano le conclusioni e decisioni che i cittadini raggiungerebbero se avessero l'occasione di discutere e dibattere approfonditamente insieme ad altri concittadini di

7 Marie Vuilleumier (2020): Durante lo stato di emergenza c'è sempre il rischio di un accaparramento eccessivo del potere. Swissinfo, 20 marzo 2020. https://www.swissinfo.ch/ita/pandemia-e-democrazia_-durante-lo-stato-di-emergenza-c-è-sempre-il-rischio-di-un-accaparramento-eccessivo-del-potere-/45632172

8 International Democracy Community (2020): Crisis councils: involving citizens in crisis management. 26 aprile 2020. https://www.democracy.community/stories/crisis-councils-involving-citizens-crisis-management

opinioni diverse. Rispetto ad un parlamento, che viene eletto in tempi più ordinari e prevedibili, un concilio di cittadini si presume essere più reattivo, comprensivo e allineato alle nuove necessità imposte dal contesto straordinario di crisi. Un simile concilio cittadino potrebbe essere utilizzato a tutti i livelli politici con due principali funzioni: fornire informazioni e consulto alle istituzioni, oppure preparare dei comunicati che spieghino alla popolazione le scelte delle istituzioni.

Altri miglioramenti si potrebbero ottenere tramite le tecnologie informatiche. Non sorprende che l'accelerazione dei processi di digitalizzazione causata dall'attuale crisi abbia riportato al centro del dibattito la questione della partecipazione online e, in particolare, del voto elettronico. Dopo alcune sperimentazioni deludenti e dopo la minaccia di una moratoria per bloccare altre sperimentazioni, il consiglio federale si è nuovamente dichiarato interessato all'argomento e-voting e ha recentemente riaperto un dialogo con esperti sul tema.[9] Se in futuro sarà possibile partecipare in modo sicuro tramite voto elettronico, la sospensione delle votazioni popolari diventerà un'opzione difficilmente percorribile anche in tempi di crisi. Al contrario, il voto elettronico potrebbe addirittura diventare uno strumento per consultare direttamente la popolazione proprio a riguardo delle crisi. Tutte queste proposte sono ambiziose, preliminari e certamente opinabili, ma se è vero che quel che non uccide fortifica, e se è vero che le istituzioni democratiche svizzere hanno retto il duro colpo del coronavirus, allora questo è il

9 Swissinfo (2020): E-Voting: rinuncia a moratoria; discussioni Confederazione-Cantoni. Swissinfo, 23 giugno 2020. https://www.swissinfo.ch/ita/e-voting--rinuncia-a-moratoria--discussioni-confederazione-cantoni/45856150

momento giusto per migliorare e fortificare il nostro sistema democratico in vista delle crisi che verranno.

9) Radikale Regierungsführung in Krisenzeiten

Raphael Capaul & Christian Ewert

In vielen demokratischen Ländern sind aktuell oder waren in den letzten Jahren politische Akteure an der Regierungsmacht, die man im weitesten Sinne als radikal bezeichnen kann. Diese Akteure zeichnen sich einerseits durch eine sehr aggressive Rhetorik aus, andererseits verfolgen sie radikale wirtschaftliche und vor allem gesellschaftliche Ziele. Dazu gehört zum Beispiel die Forderung nach einer streng geordneten und überwachten Gesellschaft, Islamophobie oder der Wunsch, aus der Europäischen Union auszutreten.

Es fällt auf, dass es vor allem diese Akteure waren, die während der letzten 12 Monate die Pandemie eher skeptisch betrachtet und Massnahmen dagegen als eher wenig dringlich eingestuft haben. Der britische Premierminister Boris Johnson hat, bis er selber an Covid19 erkrankt ist, das Virus auf die leichte Schulter genommen[1]. Trump und Bolsonaro haben ebenfalls strenge Massnahmen abgelehnt, mit der Begründung, diese würden nur der Wirtschaft schaden[2].

Die effektive Bekämpfung der Pandemie stellt Johnson, Trump, Bolsonaro und dergleichen vor grosse Herausforderungen. Dies liegt vor allem an den Eigenarten ihrer Regierungsführung, welche allein schon bei der politischen Rhetorik beginnt. Radikale Akteure behaupten geläufig, dass die Gesellschaft aus zwei sich

---

1 Spickhofen, Thomas (2020): Danach war der Ton ein anderer. Tagesschau, 02.10.2020 (https://www.tagesschau.de/ausland/johnson-covid-umgang-101.html [Stand 12.11.2020]).

2 Katsambekis, Giorgos und Stavrakakis, Yannis (2020): Populism and the Pandemic. A Collaborative Report. POPULISMUS Interventions No. 7 (special edition): Seite 6 (http://populismus.gr/wp-content/uploads/2020/06/interventions-7-populism-pandemic-UPLOAD.pdf [Stand 12.11.2020]).

gegenüberstehenden Gruppen bestehe: Auf der einen Seite das «gute, einheitliche Volk» und auf der anderen die «böse, korrupte Elite». Für jegliche gesellschaftliche Missstände konstruieren diese Akteure Sündenböcke, die verantwortlich gemacht werden. Zudem sind Tabubrüche und Provokationen, sprich ein Handeln, das nicht immer den etablierten Normen entspricht, charakteristisch für die genannten Akteure.

Das Virus selbst und der Effekt, welches es auf Wirtschaft und Gesellschaft hat, scheinen auch erstaunlich resistent gegen «fake news». Anders als wie so oft von Trump behauptet, wird es nicht «einfach verschwinden»[3]. Im Gegenteil, Trump hat sich infiziert und musste in einem Spital behandelt werden. Und die rund Dreihunderttausend Toten in den USA lassen sich ebenfalls nicht wegreden.

Auch in der Politikgestaltung scheinen sich radikale Akteure schwer zu tun. Wenn sie das Virus und seine Folgen verharmlosen, werden sie sicher keine effektiven politischen Massnahmen ergreifen können. Bedingt durch die Neuheit des Virus und dem Ausmass der Pandemie scheint auch jetzt ein weniger polarisierendes Vorgehen angemessen zu sein. Regierungen durchlaufen aktuell Lernprozesse und müssen Fehler zugeben; dies passt nicht immer zum präsentierten Selbstverständnis einiger Akteure. Laut vielen radikalen Akteuren gibt es nur eine Meinung und eine Lösung: der Wille des heraufbeschworenen «guten, einheitlichen Volkes», welcher durch sie allein vertreten wird. Wissenschaftliche Debatten und Belege werden oft ausgeblendet und diffamiert.

3 Aargauer Zeitung (2020): USA kämpfen gegen Neuinfektionen – Trump: «Virus wird verschwinden». 02.07.2020 (https://www.aargauerzeitung.ch/ausland/usa-kaempfen-gegen-neuinfektionen-trump-virus-wird-verschwinden-138332957 [Stand 12.11.2020]).

Zudem sehen sich die unterschiedlichen radikalen Akteure mit Regierungsmacht mit verschiedenen Kontexten konfrontiert, insbesondere was die Anzahl an Infektionen und die Unabhängigkeit der Medien anbelangt. Beispielsweise werden Trump und Johnson regelmässig in den nationalen Medien kritisiert. Hingegen kontrollieren die radikalen Regierungsmächte in Ungarn oder Polen die Medien viel stärker und informieren die Bevölkerung nicht umfassend über die Anzahl an Infektionen im Verhältnis zur Anzahl durchgeführter Tests und weiteren Kennwerten und deren Zusammenhang.[4] Institutionelle Kontexte können also bestimmte Handlungsstrategien begünstigen, andere hingegen verkomplizieren. Auch radikale Regierungen müssen zum einen die Handlungsmöglichkeiten erkennen und nutzen, die sich ihnen bieten, zum anderen aber mit Restriktionen und Hindernissen umgehen, welche sich ihnen entgegenstellen.

Als globales Ereignis wird die Corona-Krise sicher nicht das Ende politischer Radikalität einleiten. Aber die Krise zeigt eines deutlich: Radikale Positionen und Strategien können im Wahlkampf durchaus zum Erfolg an der Urne verhelfen; in der Regierungsführung aber, wenn es gilt, wichtige politische, wirtschaftliche und gesellschaftliche Probleme zu lösen, stösst Radikalität an ihre Grenzen.

4 Mudde, Cas (2020): Will the coronavirus 'kill populism'? Don't count on it. The Guardian, 27.03.2020 (https://www.theguardian.com/commentisfree/2020/mar/27/coronavirus-populism-trump-politics-response [Stand 12.11.2020]).

10) Demokratie in Zeiten der Pandemie: Die unterschiedlichen Reaktionen europäischer Demokratien auf die erste Welle

Palmo Brunner & Sarah Engler

Die Covid-19 Pandemie stellt mit den enormen Auswirkungen auf das gesellschaftliche Leben weltweit eine Zäsur dar. Dabei wurde sowohl im öffentlichen Diskurs als auch in der Forschung die Debatte darüber lanciert, ob Demokratien im Vergleich zu Autokratien weniger «krisenfest» seien[1]. Während Autokratien relativ frei schalten und walten können, müssen Demokratien auch in Krisen die Einschränkung von individuellen Freiheitsrechten rechtfertigen. Insbesondere werden Demokratien mit dem Dilemma konfrontiert, inwiefern Massnahmen zum Schutz der öffentlichen Gesundheit andere demokratische Prinzipien untergraben dürfen. Zum einen führt der Druck, schnell reagieren zu können, zu einer Machtkonzentration zu Gunsten der nationalen Regierung, zum anderen enthalten die konkreten Massnahmen des «Social Distancing» Einschränkungen fundamentaler Rechte wie die der Bewegungs- und Versammlungsfreiheit. In Krisenzeiten können Eingriffe in die Grundrechte als legitim gelten, solange diese notwendig, verhältnismässig, zeitlich begrenzt und nicht diskriminierend sind. Dabei besteht jedoch ein erheblicher Spielraum. Dies zeigte sich darin, dass es in der ersten Welle der Covid-19 Pandemie nicht nur Unterschiede zwischen Demokratien und Autokratien gab, sondern auch innerhalb der Demokratien Europas. Mit einer ähnlichen Bedrohungslage konfrontiert,

1 Cheibub, Jose Antonio, Hong, Ji Yeon Jean and Przeworski, Adam (2020): Rights and Deaths: Government Reactions to the Pandemic. Working Paper (https://ssrn.com/abstract=3645410 [Stand 30.11.2020]).

entschieden sich manche Länder für weitreichende, andere für mildere Einschränkungen der demokratischen Prinzipien.

Eine interdisziplinäre Forschungsgruppe an der Universität Zürich hat deshalb untersucht, wie europäische Demokratien in der ersten Welle der Pandemie mit dem bereits beschriebenen Dilemma umgegangen sind und wie sich die verschiedenen Reaktionen erklären lassen[2]. Ein wichtiger Faktor dabei ist, dass in demokratischen Ländern – auch wenn in Zeiten der Krise zunächst Kontrollmechanismen ausgehebelt werden können – die Regierungen im Nachhinein zur Rechenschaft gezogen werden können. Politische Entscheidungsträger antizipieren deshalb, dass die verhängten Massnahmen von Stimmbürgerinnen und -bürgern, den Gerichten, dem Parlament sowie zivilgesellschaftlichen Organisationen auf ihre Legitimität und Verhältnismässigkeit hinterfragt und angefochten werden können. So haben in Deutschland beispielsweise die Verwaltungsgerichte bereits einige Beschränkungen wieder gekippt. Unsere Analyse zeigt auf, dass sich die Unterschiede zwischen den europäischen Demokratien tatsächlich nicht nur aufgrund von pandemierelevanten Faktoren erklären lassen, sondern auch entscheidend ist, inwiefern demokratische Prinzipien und Institutionen in «normalen Zeiten» bereits in einem Land verankert waren. Dabei fokussieren wir uns auf zwei Dimensionen des demokratischen Dilemmas: Die Machtkonzentration in den Händen der Exekutive und die Einschränkungen von individuellen Freiheiten.

---

2 Engler, Sarah, Brunner, Palmo, Loviat, Romane, Abou-Chadi, Tarik, Leeman, Lucas, Glaser, Andreas & Kübler, Daniel (2020): Democracy in times of the pandemic: Explaining the variation of public health policies against COVID-19 across European democracies. Universität Zürich (unveröffentlichtes Manuskript).

Bei der Machtkonzentration ist auffällig, dass vor allem in osteuropäischen Ländern wie Serbien oder Ungarn die Parlamente teilweise entmachtet wurden. Auch die Medien als die vierte Gewalt in der Demokratie waren mit vielen Restriktionen konfrontiert. Erstaunlicherweise ist auch die Schweiz eines der wenigen westeuropäischen Länder, welches bedeutend die Macht auf die nationale Exekutive konzentrierte. Zum einen unterbrach das Schweizer Parlament zu Beginn der Pandemie seine Session und tagte erst später wieder, zum anderen wurden viele Kompetenzen der Kantone auf den Bundesrat übertragen. Bereits das Ausrufen der «Ausserordentlichen Lage» wurde nicht, wie in den meisten Ländern Westeuropas üblich, durch das Parlament legitimiert. Im Bereich der Einschränkungen der individuellen Freiheiten in der ersten Welle sind Serbien sowie Bosnien und Herzegowina an der Spitze, wo strikte Ausgangssperren verordnet und auch Ansammlungen von kleinen Gruppen untersagt wurden. Aber auch Länder wie Spanien, Frankreich oder Italien schränkten die Bewegungsfreiheit stark ein. Auf der anderen Seite befinden sich Island, Finnland und Schweden mit relativ milden Massnahmen. Es zeigt sich ein klarer Trend: In Ländern, in denen der Schutz der individuellen Freiheiten stark verankert ist, waren Regierungen in der ersten Welle in der Regel zögerlicher im Umgang mit freiheitsbeschränkenden Massnahmen.

In der ersten Welle der Pandemie hielten also jene Länder den Schutz der individuellen Freiheit hoch, die diesen auch sonst stark gewichten. Auf der anderen Seite können Zeiten der Unsicherheiten in Ländern mit tiefer oder sinkender Demokratiequalität genutzt werden, um weiter demokratische

Rückschritte einzuleiten[3]. Auch wenn wir in unserer Studie nicht den Erfolg der Massnahmen zur Pandemie-Bekämpfung untersuchen, zeigt sich, dass Regierungen in den stabilen Demokratien Europas demokratische Lösungen auf die Pandemie finden müssen, insbesondere damit die Akzeptanz für freiheitseinschränkende Regelungen in der Bevölkerung weiterhin bestehen bleibt.

3 Lührmann, Anna, Amanda B. Edgell, Sandra Grahn, Jean Lachapelle, and Seraphine F. Maerz (2020). Does the Coronavirus Endanger Democracy in Europe? Carnegie Europe (https://carnegieeurope.eu/2020/06/23/does-coronavirus-endanger-democracy-in-europe-pub-82110 [Stand 30.11.2020]).

11) Machtverschiebung zwischen Exekutive und Legislative in Krisenzeiten

Raphael Capaul

Für eine Demokratie und einen Rechtsstaat ist es grundlegend, dass Institutionen und deren Funktionen so angeordnet werden, dass staatliche Macht beschränkt und deren Missbrauch verhindert wird. Alle demokratischen Staaten, wie auch die Schweiz, sind nach dem Prinzip der Gewaltenteilung (Exekutive, Legislative und Judikative) organisiert. So ist das Verhältnis zwischen Exekutive und Legislative eine wichtige Charakteristik eines Landes.[1] In der Schweiz bildet die vereinigte Bundesversammlung (das Parlament), bestehend aus den beiden gleichgestellten Kammern National- und Ständerat, die Legislative. Der Bundesrat (die Regierung), welchem die öffentliche Verwaltung direkt untersteht, bildet die Exekutive.[2]

Gemäss der Bundesverfassung übt die Bundesversammlung unter Vorbehalt von Volk und Ständen «die oberste Gewalt im Bund» aus. Die Bundesversammlung hat somit formal eine starke Stellung, beziehungsweise eine Vorrangstellung gegenüber der Regierung.[3] In Anbetracht der faktischen Kontrollmöglichkeiten der Bundesversammlung gegenüber der Regierung gilt es aber, die starke Position der Bundesversammlung zu relativieren. Die Informations- und Kontrollressourcen des Milizparlaments gelten als begrenzt.[4]

1 Vatter, Adrian (2020): Das politische System der Schweiz. Baden-Baden: Nomos, S. 301.

2 Vatter, Adrian (2020), S. 407.

3 Glaser, Andreas und Gfeller, Katja (2020): Das Ringen des Parlaments um mehr Macht: Rückschlag infolge der Corona-Pandemie? Jusletter, 5. Oktober 2020, S. 2-3; Vatter, Adrian (2020), S. 266.

4 Vatter, Adrian (2020), S. 301-305.

Trotzdem konnte die Bundesversammlung in den vergangenen Jahren und Jahrzehnten in verschiedenen Bereichen ihre Macht ausbauen.[5] Beispielsweise sind die parlamentarischen Aktivitäten in den letzten 20 Jahren stark angestiegen[6] und die Kontrollfunktion der Bundesversammlung gegenüber der Regierung konnte in den letzten 50 Jahren schrittweise ausgebaut werden.[7]

Es steht in der Kompetenz des Bundesrates, in Notlagen Notrecht zu erlassen.[8] Für die Bewältigung von Krisen ist ein rasches, flexibles und effektives Handeln notwendig. Die Exekutive wird diesen Anforderungen besser gerecht, da sie im Vergleich zur Legislative kleiner ist und sich regelmässiger trifft. Machtverschiebungen hin zur Exekutive sind dementsprechend für Krisenzeiten typisch – in Krisenzeiten schlägt die Stunde der Exekutive. In solchen besonderen Umständen, in denen Grundrechte und Freiheiten per sofort eingeschränkt werden, ist deshalb die gegenseitige Kontrolle der Gewalten von besonderer Wichtigkeit.[9]

Die Exekutive kann während Krisenzeiten das Parlament in Entscheidungsprozesse einbeziehen. Das Parlament ist wichtig für die demokratische Legitimation von getroffenen Massnahmen. Es kann darüber debattieren, ob die

---

5 Glaser, Andreas und Gfeller, Katja (2020); Vatter, Adrian (2020), S. 261 ff.

6 Brüschweiler, Jonas und Vatter, Adrian (2018): Viele Vorstösse, wenig Wirkung? Nutzung und Erfolg parlamentarischer Instrumente in der Bundesversammlung, in: Adrian Vatter (Hrsg.). Das Parlament in der Schweiz. Macht und Ohnmacht der Volksvertretung. NZZ Libro: Zürich, S. 69-99.

7 Vatter, Adrian (2020), S. 295.

8 Glaser, Andreas und Gfeller, Katja (2020), S. 4; Lienhard, Andreas und Kettiger, Daniel (2020): Justiz in Krisenzeiten. Justice – Justiz – Giustizia 2020/2, S. 2-4.

9 Glaser, Andreas und Gfeller, Katja (2020), S. 15; Griglio, Elena (2020): Parliamentary oversight under the Covid-19 emergency: striving against executive dominance. The Theory and Practice of Legislation 8(1-2): 49-70; Uhlmann, Felix und Scheifele, Eva (2020): Legislative response to Coronavirus (Switzerland). The Theory and Practice of Legislation 8(1-2): 115-130.

Notmassnahmen der Exekutive angemessen und notwendig sind.[10]

Die Corona-Krise hat international[11], wie auch in der Schweiz, zu einer Machtverschiebung von der Legislative hin zur Exekutive geführt. Die Schweizer Bundesversammlung brach am 15. März 2020 ihre laufende und ordentliche Session frühzeitig ab. Am 16. März verkündete der Bundesrat die ausserordentliche Lage gemäss dem Epidemiengesetz und erliess daraufhin zahlreiche Notverordnungen. Die Bundesversammlung hatte für über eineinhalb Monate im Frühjahr 2020 lediglich eine Rolle als Zuschauerin inne. Erst am 4. Mai 2020 traf sie sich wieder für eine ausserordentliche Corona-Session und korrigierte die Notverordnungen des Bundesrates nicht.[12]

Die Bundesversammlung stellte im Frühjahr 2020 ihre Arbeit für mehrere Wochen komplett ein. Diese abrupte und extreme Machtverschiebung von der Legislative zur Exekutive stellt den Machtzugewinn der Legislative in den vergangenen Jahren wieder in Frage.

10 Griglio, Elena (2020), S. 52-53.

11 Griglio, Elena (2020).

12 Glaser, Andreas und Gfeller, Katja (2020), S. 16; Uhlmann, Felix und Scheifele, Eva (2020), S. 121-122.

12) Expert:innen an die Macht? Covid-19 und die Technokratisierung der Politik

Lea Heyne

Dass Anders Tegnell, Staatspidemologe und Vorsitzender der schwedischen Gesundheitsbehörde *Folkhälsomyndigheten*, einmal zum Tattoomotiv würde, hätte er sich vermutlich nicht träumen lassen. Doch im April 2020 gelangte ein junger Schwede in die Schlagzeilen, der sich Tegnells Konterfei auf seinem Arm verewigen ließ. Das ist nur die Spitze des Eisbergs: Auf sozialen Medien sammeln sich Fanseiten, Accounts und Unterstützergruppen für Tegnell, Fans des Virologen tragen T-Shirts und andere Memorabilien mit der Aufschrift "Alle Macht für Tegnell, unseren Befreier". Schwedische Medien kürten ihn bereits zum neuen „Landesvater".[1] Und Tegnell ist nicht der einzige Wissenschaftler, der in den letzten Monaten gewollt oder ungewollt zum Volkshelden wurde: In Deutschland titelte die Wochenzeitung „Die Zeit" über Christian Drosten, leitender Virologe an der Charité Berlin, „Ist das unser neuer Kanzler?"[2] Auch Drosten wird in den sozialen Medien zum Teil wie ein Popstar gefeiert, gleichzeitig erhält er nach eigenen Angaben inzwischen aber auch regelmäßig Hassnachrichten und persönliche Bedrohungen. Ähnlich ging es in den USA Anthony Fauci, führender Forscher für Infektionskrankheiten, der als Mitglied der Coronavirus-Taskforce des Weißen Hauses zwischen die Fronten eines erbitterten politischen Kampfes geriet: Während Demokraten ihn als Helden und Rächer feiern, verlangten Trump und führende Republikaner immer wieder seinen Rücktritt und

---

1 https://theconversation.com/coronavirus-has-put-scientists-in-the-frame-alongside-politicians-and-poses-questions-about-leadership-148498

2 https://www.zeit.de/2020/13/coronavirus-wissenschaft-auswirkung-auf-politik-virologen-christian-drosten-alexander-kekule

warfen ihm Lügen vor, er steht aufgrund massiver Drohungen mittlerweile mit seiner gesamten Familie unter Polizeischutz[3].

Mit der Corona-Pandemie sind Expert:innnen, insbesondere im Bereich der Virologie, plötzlich ins Zentrum des politischen Geschehens und der öffentlichen Meinung gerückt. Wissenschaftler:innen erklären den Bürger:innen die Pandemie und beraten Regierungen. Wissenschaftliche Verfahren, seien es PCR-Tests, verschiedene Impftechnologien oder die Peer-Review für wissenschaftliche Publikationen sind im Alltagswissen angekommen. Fragt man in Bevölkerungsumfragen, wem die Menschen am meisten vertrauen, schneiden Expert:innen grundsätzlich deutlich besser ab als Politiker:innen – diese Tendenz hat die Covid-19 Pandemie noch einmal verstärkt. Eine nachvollziehbare, aber nicht unproblematische Entwicklung, denn auch wenn in Krisenzeiten Expertise noch wichtiger ist als sonst, droht damit auch eine Verwischung der Grenzen zwischen Politik und Wissenschaft.

Einerseits durch eine *Technokratisierung der Politik*, wobei politische Entscheidungen aufgrund von Expertise getroffen werden[4]. Denn Demokratie basiert darauf, dass Entscheidungen durch Wahlen legitimiert, beziehungsweise von durch Wahlen legitimierten Politiker:innen getroffen werden. Technokratie hingegen bedeutet eine Legitimation durch Expertenwissen, und damit eine De-Politisierung der Politik. Denn anders als politische Debatten, in denen es um rechts oder links, konservativ oder liberal gehen kann, basiert eine technokratische Entscheidungsfindung

3 https://www.cnbc.com/2020/08/05/dr-fauci-says-his-daughters-need-security-as-family-continues-to-get-death-threats.html

4 Siehe z.B. Bertsou/Caramani (2020): The Technocratic Challenge to Democracy, Routledge.

auf der Annahme, dass es schlicht eine „richtige" und eine „falsche" Vorgehensweise gibt, und man nur die richtigen Expert:innen fragen muss, um ein Problem zu lösen. Dieses zutiefst wissenschaftliche Prinzip – die Suche nach der Wahrheit – ist zwar elementar wichtig für moderne Demokratien, doch darf es nicht das demokratische Prinzip ersetzen. Wissenschaftler:innen und Expert:innen dürfen und müssen Regierungen beraten, insbesondere während einer Ausnahmesituation wie der Corona-Pandemie, aber Expert:innen können immer nur wissenschaftliche Ratschläge geben, aber keine politischen Maßnahmen begründen. Dafür braucht es demokratisch legitimierte und gewählte Politiker:innen, und politisch begründete Maßnahmen. In einer Demokratie muss jede Entscheidung debattierbar und anfechtbar sein, auch und gerade, wenn sie auf objektiv richtiger Expertise basiert. Im Gegensatz zu Anders Tegnell, der ohne direkte demokratische Legitimation zum politischen Chefstrategen des schwedischen „Sonderweges" geworden ist, wissen Christian Drosten und Anthony Fauci übrigens durchaus um diesen Unterscheid. Beide haben wiederholt betont, dass sie keine politischen Entscheidungen treffen können oder wollen, sondern rein wissenschaftlich und beratend agieren.

Die Kehrseite einer zunehmenden Technokratisierung der Demokratie, und nicht minder problematisch, ist eine *Politisierung der Wissenschaft*: Insbesondere in den USA, aber auch unter europäischen Corona-Kritikern konnte man in den letzten Monaten beobachten, wie objektive wissenschaftliche Erkenntnisse als politische Meinungen behandelt werden, die zur Debatte stehen. Nicht nur Verschwörungstheoretiker, sondern auch gewählte Politiker wie Trump oder Bolsonaro, leugnen öffentlich Fakten und greifen Wissenschaftler:innen an, indem sie ihnen Parteilichkeit und eine politische Agenda unterstellen. Diese Tendenz, wissenschaftliche Erkenntnisse und Fakten als Propaganda abzutun, ist nicht neu (man denke an die Debatte um den menschengemachten Klimawandel), aber hat während der Corona-Pandemie einen traurigen Höhepunkt erreicht, wie man an den massiven Drohungen gegen Wissenschaftler:innen wie Fauci und Drosten sieht, die gegen ihren Willen zu politischen Akteuren erklärt werden, die sie gar nicht sein wollen.

Beide Tendenzen sind also gefährlich für eine Demokratie – einerseits eine Technokratisierung und Ent-Politisierung von Politik, andererseits eine Politisierung von Wissenschaft, die mit dem Leugnen von Fakten einhergeht. Damit unsere Demokratien die Corona-Krise unbeschadet überstehen, ist es daher wichtig, dass wir das wissenschaftliche Prinzip von „wahr“ oder „falsch“ aus der Politik heraushalten, und umgekehrt politische Debatten nicht um die Richtigkeit, sondern um die demokratische Interpretation wissenschaftlicher Erkenntnisse führen. In Schweden jedenfalls scheint sich das Blatt für Tegnell zum ersten Mal zu wenden: Ende November drängte Ministerpräsident Löfven ihn unerwartet aus dem Rampenlicht, indem er parallel zu Tegnells wöchentlichem Auftritt eigene Pressenkonferenz einberief und dort im Lichte der zweiten Infektionswelle strengere Auflagen ankündigte, als Tegnell es empfohlen hatte. Ein erstes Zeichen einer Wende von technokratischen zu demokratischen Entscheidungen? Man möchte es hoffen.

13) Le lobbying en temps de pandémie : quelques réflexions sur une pratique en pleine mutation

Odile Ammann

S'il existe une règle d'or en matière de lobbying, c'est bien celle-là : l'entretien en face-à-face doit être privilégié, car c'est l'une des méthodes de persuasion les plus efficaces. Bien plus qu'un e-mail, un coup de fil ou l'envoi de documentation, un rendez-vous en personne permet aux groupes d'intérêt de gagner la confiance de leur vis-à-vis, d'exposer leurs doléances aux autorités et de réagir immédiatement aux propos et aux signaux non-verbaux de leurs interlocutrices et interlocuteurs. Le lobbying est une pratique inscrite dans un espace donné, comme le démontre son étymologie qui se réfère à l'antichambre du parlement. Faire du lobbying signifie investir les espaces où citoyen-ne-s et politicien-ne-s peuvent se rencontrer.

Comme nous ne le savons que trop bien, la pandémie de Covid-19 a révolutionné notre rapport collectif à l'espace public, devenu un vivier d'infections. Afin d'infléchir la courbe des contagions, les autorités ont fortement limité les rassemblements de personnes, y compris en Suisse. Même si ces restrictions ont – après quelques hésitations de la part de l'Office fédéral de la justice – été déclarées inapplicables aux réunions parlementaires, les mesures d'hygiène et de distanciation sociale n'ont pas manqué d'affecter le travail législatif ainsi que les interactions des parlementaires avec les groupes d'intérêt. Cette mutation a également contaminé – mutatis mutandis – le pouvoir exécutif.

Or, si les rencontres physiques ont été drastiquement réduites, le lobbying n'a pas disparu de la surface, bien au contraire.

Dans les pays où de telles données sont disponibles, comme aux États-Unis ou au Canada, de premières recherches révèlent que les dépenses des groupes d'intérêt pour leurs activités de lobbying ont atteint de nouveaux sommets, comme si ces chiffres voulaient rivaliser avec les courbes vertigineuses des infections.

Cette hyperactivité n'est pas une surprise. En effet, en plus de contraindre les lobbys à adapter leur stratégie de persuasion en abandonnant ou en réduisant fortement les interactions en présence et les événements publics, la pandémie a aussi provoqué la mise en place d'une vague de mesures qui touchent directement et souvent lourdement les groupes d'intérêt. Songeons par exemple au secteur de l'aviation, au tourisme, aux transports publics ou encore au sport professionnel, dont les activités ont été limitées de manière significative par les mesures sanitaires. La résolution des problèmes créés par ces mesures dépend en grande partie de la volonté des autorités publiques. Par conséquent, si certaines voix décrient le fait que la pandémie a provoqué une véritable « épidémie » de lobbying, celle-ci n'est guère surprenante, contrairement au coronavirus qui a pris de court le monde entier, y compris les démocraties libérales.

Les groupes d'intérêt ne se retrouvent pas sur un pied d'égalité en période de pandémie : leur capacité d'agir dépend de manière significative des ressources dont ils disposent. De plus, les membres de ces organisations doivent s'adapter à la crise et travailler dans des conditions plus ou moins propices. La rapidité de réaction est d'autant plus importante dans le contexte d'une situation épidémiologique et politique évoluant sans cesse, où les délais de consultation fixés par les autorités sont souvent fortement raccourcis.

Pendant les premiers mois de la crise, le lobbying s'est concentré sur l'exécutif. Pour citer un exemple, à la mi-avril, le Tages-Anzeiger rapportait que le président de GastroSuisse, la fédération nationale de l'hôtellerie et de la restauration, avait envoyé un courriel aux cinq représentant-e-s des partis bourgeois au sein du Conseil fédéral pour les prier de défendre les intérêts de sa branche en permettant une réouverture rapide des restaurants[1]. Cette stratégie frontale a été critiquée par plusieurs personnes du métier.

Afin d'éviter que les groupes d'intérêt ne soient exclus du processus décisionnel en lien avec les mesures prises par les autorités, ces dernières ont parfois décidé d'associer directement certains acteurs au processus décisionnel. Ainsi, l'organisation faîtière des entreprises Économiesuisse a-t-elle trouvé place dans l'État-major du Conseil fédéral chargé de gérer la crise du coronavirus. En revanche, parmi les absent-e-s, on compte notamment l'Association suisse des infirmiers et infirmières et la Fédération suisse pour l'accueil de jour de l'enfant, ainsi que les représentant-e-s du personnel médical, ou encore les milieux culturels et artistiques. Comme le relève la politologue danoise Anne Rasmussen dans une étude préliminaire, les consultations fermées – comme celles qui ont lieu au sein de l'Etat-major – comportent le risque que de nombreux acteurs ne puissent pas participer au processus délibératif[2]. Toutefois, ces processus peuvent aussi permettre à des organisations aux ressources modestes de participer plus activement que lors d'une consultation ouverte. Au sein de l'Union européenne, Rasmussen constate une forte présence des milieux économiques dans les réunions des membres

1 Markus Häfliger, 'Wie die Gastrolobby Alain Berset ausmanövrieren wollte', Tages-Anzeiger, 17 avril 2020.

2 Anne Rasmussen, 'How Has Covid-19 Changed Lobbying Activity Across Europe?', LSE EUROPP blog, 17 juin 2020.

de la Commission européenne (Commissaires et haut-e-s fonctionnaires de la Commission) dédiées à la gestion de la pandémie, que ces réunions soient digitales ou non. Toutefois, cette situation ne diffère pas de manière marquée de celle observée avant la pandémie.

Par ailleurs, la digitalisation a subi une accélération sans précédent depuis le début de la propagation du coronavirus, y compris dans le domaine de la politique. En mars 2020, le Parlement fédéral a, pour la première fois dans son histoire, interrompu sa session de printemps, considérant que le risque de contagion était devenu trop élevé. Il a ensuite tenu deux sessions (l'une extraordinaire, l'autre ordinaire) en dehors du Palais fédéral, dans le bâtiment de Bernexpo, afin de permettre le respect des recommandations de l'Office fédéral de la santé publique en termes d'hygiène et de distanciation sociale[3]. Afin de s'adapter à ces contraintes, les parlementaires ont notamment, selon leurs propres dires, « multiplié les groupes WhatsApp pour pouvoir échanger » entre eux[4]. On peut imaginer que de tels canaux de communication informels ont également été établis entre représentants politiques et lobbyistes, ces derniers s'étant vu refuser l'accès au Palais fédéral et aux locaux de Bernexpo pendant plusieurs mois.

S'il a d'innombrables conséquences néfastes, le coronavirus a aussi accéléré les innovations démocratiques, y compris en matière de lobbying. La plateforme « Crowd-Lobbying », lancée par Daniel Graf quelques mois avant le début de la pandémie et renforcée depuis lors, permet aux citoyen-ne-s d'influencer

---

3 Pour une évaluation juridique de la réaction du Parlement fédéral à la pandémie, voir Odile Ammann/Felix Uhlmann, 'Switzerland: The (Missing) Role of Parliament in Times of Crisis', sous presse.

4 Eric Felley, 'Un marathon de folie pour les parlementaires', lematin.ch, 6 mai 2020.

les parlementaires membres de commissions en leur transmettant des souhaits liés à un dossier précis par internet.

La technologie est souvent considérée comme un instrument de démocratisation. Toutefois, elle peut aussi renforcer des inégalités préexistantes. Un groupe d'intérêt disposant d'un épais carnet d'adresses peut y avoir recours même en l'absence de réunions physiques. Rasmussen constate que les acteurs économiques constituent une très large proportion des entités participant à des réunions digitales avec la Commission européenne. En revanche, une organisation ne disposant guère de tels points d'accès peinera d'autant plus à établir de telles relations dans un contexte où les rencontres en présentiel sont proscrites. En outre, les rencontres digitales sont moins à même d'établir une relation de confiance qu'une rencontre physique lorsqu'il s'agit de la première prise de contact. Une étude empirique menée par des politologues de l'Université de Copenhague, du Trinity College Dublin et de l'Université d'Amsterdam démontre qu'au sein de l'Union européenne ainsi que dans neuf pays européens, les ONG ont diminué leurs activités de lobbying de manière marquée, contrairement aux organisations économiques et professionnelles, qui ont augmenté ces activités[5].

En Suisse, de nombreuses voix ont réclamé la création de bases légales permettant au Parlement fédéral et à ses commissions de siéger virtuellement[6]. Ces réflexions n'en sont encore qu'à leurs balbutiements. Plusieurs questions se posent dans ce contexte, y compris en matière de lobbying.

5 Wiebke Marie Junk/Michele Crepaz/Marcel Hanegraaff/Joost Berkhout/Ellis Aizenberg, 'Interest Representation During the Corona Virus Crisis: Results From the European Union and Nine European Countries', septembre 2020.

6 Voir p.ex. Doris Fialla, interpellation 20.3098, 'Coronavirus. Un Parlement virtuel serait-il une solution ?', 11 mars 2020.

Par exemple, comment garantir une délibération de qualité dans un environnement digital ? Dans un article publié dans la Neue Zürcher Zeitung à la fin du mois de novembre, Remo Hess notait qu'au sein des autorités elles-mêmes, les réunions digitales – qu'il qualifie de « Zoom-Diplomatie » – empêchaient plus encore que d'habitude la formation de compromis[7]. Tel est notamment le cas du Conseil européen, constitué des chefs d'État des pays membres de l'Union européenne, où les représentants polonais et hongrois font bloc contre le budget et le plan de relance européens. Il y a lieu de présumer que de telles difficultés se posent aussi en lien avec les interventions des représentants d'intérêts. Pour revenir à la Suisse, une autre question concerne les séances des commissions parlementaires, dont la confidentialité doit être assurée en toutes circonstances. Comment respecter cette exigence lorsque les réunions ont lieu virtuellement ? Enfin, et il s'agit probablement là de la question la plus importante, comment faire en sorte que les représentants d'intérêts jouissent d'un accès égal aux politicien-ne-s dans l'espace virtuel ? Il y a lieu d'espérer que les projets en cours en matière de parlement digital jouent un rôle pionnier en la matière. Ils pourraient alors inspirer, à leur tour, le droit parlementaire applicable aux réunions en présence, où de nombreux efforts restent encore à fournir.

7 Remo Hess, 'Zoom-Diplomatie verhindert Kompromisse', NZZ am Sonntag, 29 novembre 2020.

14) Unterschriftensammlungen in Zeiten des «Social Distancing»

Flavia Caroni

Anfang März 2020 sprachen die Behörden in europäischen Ländern erstmals eine neue, bisher unbekannte Empfehlung zur Erhaltung der Gesundheit aus: Abstand halten. Halten Sie jederzeit einen Abstand von zwei Metern zu anderen Personen ein, und vermeiden Sie grössere Menschenansammlungen, wurde den Einwohnerinnen der Schweiz eingeschärft. Kurz darauf wurden solche Ansammlungen behördlich untersagt. Die Menschen sollten sich so wenig wie möglich begegnen. Dieses «Social Distancing» und die Angst vor einer Ansteckung dürften es sein, die die «Corona»-Erfahrung für viele Menschen am meisten prägt, übertroffen nur von den wirtschaftlichen Nöten, in die die Pandemie so manche zu stürzen droht.

Für eine Institution, die von direkten Kontakten zwischen Menschen lebt, kann dies zu einem grossen Problem werden: die direkte Demokratie. Die offensichtlichen Einschränkungen ihrer Grundrechte und politischen Rechte, die die Bürger demokratischer Länder aufgrund der Pandemie hinnehmen mussten, werden an anderer Stelle in diesem Buch thematisiert. Auch die teils freiwilligen Verhaltensänderungen der Menschen aber treffen das öffentlich-politische Leben hart und zwingen es auf Sparflamme. Gerade in der Schweiz mit ihren ausgebauten direktdemokratischen Institutionen kommt diesem eine besondere Bedeutung zu. Vorträge, Podien, Filmvorführungen und Apéros, die sonst ein engagiertes Publikum anzogen, wenn auch nicht immer ein grosses, werden in den digitalen Raum verlegt oder gar nicht erst angesetzt. Jene, die physisch stattfinden, müssen dies vor halbleeren Rängen tun, oder stossen angesichts der herrschenden Besorgnis auf wenig Echo.

Unmittelbar und spürbar darunter leiden tut die direkte Demokratie Schweizer Art insbesondere, da ihre wichtigsten Instrumente auf Unterschriftensammlungen beruhen. Zwar verfügte der Bundesrat vom 20. März bis Ende Mai 2020 einen Fristenstillstand für Initiativen und Referenden, eine weitreichende Massnahme, die seit Einführung der Instrumente im 19. Jahrhundert noch nie ergriffen worden war. Seit Juni 2020 aber müssen sich die Komitees wieder um Unterschriften bemühen, damit die Sammelfristen ihrer Anliegen nicht ungenutzt ablaufen. Wie schwierig das ist, zeigt sich an der im Vergleich zu den Vorjahren sehr geringen Anzahl lancierter und eingereichter Initiativen und Referenden im Jahr 2020. Das Ziel von Volksinitiativen ist generell, neue Anliegen auf die politische Agenda zu bringen oder bei bestehenden politischen Regelungen Korrekturen zu bewirken. Bei ihnen dürfte nach Ende der Pandemie mit einem gewissen Nachhol-Effekt zu rechnen sein – sie können, bis zu einem gewissen Grad, warten. Anders sieht es bei Referenden aus, da diese unmittelbar als Reaktion auf parlamentarische Beschlüsse ergriffen werden müssen. Hier ist damit zu rechnen, dass die direkte Mitsprache der Stimmbürgerinnen und Stimmbürger in Zeiten der Pandemie eingeschränkt ist.

Anlässe politischer Parteien und Verbände wie auch zivilgesellschaftlicher Organisationen sind normalerweise wichtige Orte der Kontaktaufnahme zwischen bereits engagierten Bürgerinnen und Interessierten, wo letztere für ein Engagement gewonnen werden können – ein Engagement wie jenes, für eine Initiative oder ein Referendum Unterschriften zu sammeln. Der Politikwissenschaft ist die

Bedeutung persönlicher Beziehungen und Kontakte für dieses sogenannte «Recruitment» schon lange bekannt.[1]
Nebst Möglichkeiten zu Austausch, Vernetzung und eben Rekrutierung sind es natürlich die Möglichkeiten zur Unterschriftensammlung selbst, die fehlen. Ein grosser Teil der Unterschriften wird nach wie vor im öffentlichen Raum gesammelt, «auf der Strasse». Eben diese Strassen sind in Zeiten der Pandemie deutlich weniger bevölkert als normalerweise, und wer unterwegs ist, ist oft noch verschlossener als ohnehin schon. Für meine Forschung[2] interviewe ich Personen, die in zentralen Rollen an Unterschriftensammlungen für Volksinitiativen beteiligt waren. Sie berichten von Passanten, die angesichts von Fremden, die sich ihnen nähern, zurückweichen, von Bürgerinnen, die keinen Unterschriftenbogen, keinen Stift, kein Klemmbrett anfassen mögen, das vorher schon jemand anderes berührt hat.

Während viele Arbeitgeber angesichts der Notwendigkeit des «Social Distancing» sehr schnell auf Homeoffice umgestellt und die Arbeitswelt in der Folge einen kräftigen Digitalisierungsschub erfahren hat, ist ein solcher bei der Demokratie schwieriger zu erreichen. Da die E-Unterschrift, wie auch das E-Voting, noch in eher ferner Zukunft liegen, muss die Unterschrift letztlich immer mit Stift auf Papier erfolgen. Dies erhöht die Kosten einer Unterschrift für die potentiell angesprochenen Bürgerinnen deutlich:

1 Siehe zum Beispiel: Schlozman, Kay Lehman; Verba, Sidney; Brady, Henry E. (1999): Civic Participation and the Equality Problem. S. 427–459 in: Theda Skocpol und Morris P. Fiorina (Hg.): Civic engagement in American democracy. Washington, D.C., Great Britain, New York: Brookings Institution Press; Russell Sage Foundation,

2 Die Forschung im Rahmen eines Dissertationsprojekts am Institut für Politikwissenschaft der Universität Zürich unter dem Arbeitstitel «Strategien und Aktivitäten im Initiativprozess» ist noch unveröffentlicht.

Wo auf der Strasse in weniger als einer Minute und mit wenig gedanklichem Aufwand die nötigen Angaben eingetragen sind, muss zuhause ein Drucker vorhanden sein, ein Umschlag, eine Briefmarke, um aus einem PDF einen verwertbaren Unterschriftenbogen zu machen. Die Eifrigen und Überzeugten mag das nicht abhalten, die Verhaltensökonomie lässt aber keine Zweifel daran, dass bereits kleine Hürden viele Menschen von ihren Vorhaben abbringen können.

Initiativen und Referenden, deren Unterschriftensammlung primär mit digitalen Mitteln organisiert und durchgeführt wurde, zum Beispiel mittels der Unterschriftenplattform «WeCollect», sind bis heute eine Seltenheit. In der Regel dienen digitale Mittel als Ergänzung zu den klassischen Kampagneninstrumenten. Dabei sind es eher E-Mails, die in der Unterschriftensammlung zentral sind, erklären mir meine Interviewpartner, als die heute so prominenten sozialen Medien – letztere gewinnen erst in der Abstimmungskampagne an Bedeutung. E-Mail-Adressen sind denn auch eine wichtige Währung in der digitalen Unterschriftensammlung. Wer eine Datenbank mit tausenden davon hat, gar zehntausenden oder mehr, kann diese effektiv nutzen. Eine solche Datenbank entsteht aber nicht über Nacht, sondern muss über Jahre aufgebaut werden. Während der physische öffentliche Raum es erlaubt, zufällig Fremde anzusprechen, und ein politischer Anlass mit einem grosszügigen Apéro auch Interessierte ohne bestehende Beziehungen zu den Organisatorinnen anlocken kann, sind im digitalen Raum erst einmal nur jene erreichbar, zu denen schon Verbindungen bestehen. Nur wenige politische Anliegen sind so attraktiv, treffen den Nerv der Zeit und der Stimmberechtigten so genau, dass sie es vermögen, eine

Eigendynamik zu entwickeln, die es ermöglicht, dass sie gewissermassen von selbst weiter gestreut werden.

Im Gegensatz zur Arbeitswelt, in der in vielen Bereichen die physische durch eine digitale Zusammenarbeit recht gut ersetzt werden konnte, bleibt die direkte Demokratie Schweizer Art also auf physische Interaktion angewiesen. Entsprechend stark wirkt sich das «Social Distancing» auf sie aus. Dennoch würde ich argumentieren, dass die direkte Demokratie in der Schweiz robust ist. Die Institutionen haben in ihrer Geschichte schon viel Wandel überstanden, und die Identifikation der Bürgerinnen und Bürger mit der direkten Demokratie ist hoch. Auf eine vollständige Erholung der Patientin nach überstandener Pandemie darf also durchaus gehofft werden.

15) Democrazia deliberativa nell'epoca del Covid-19

Francesco Veri

Il Covid-19 è un temibile virus, ma anche e soprattutto sinonimo di crisi sanitaria, crisi economica, crisi sociale e crisi politica. I governi di tutto il mondo hanno cercato soluzioni per affrontare le conseguenze del Covid-19, senza però aver identificato la formula perfetta che sappia arginare i danni provocati alla salute, e allo stesso tempo rispettare l'integrità del sistema democratico. Questa breve riflessione intende analizzare le conseguenze del Covid-19 sul sistema democratico attraverso le lenti della cosiddetta democrazia deliberativa, ovvero la teoria democratica che mette al centro del sistema il dibattito e la comunicazione.

Democrazia deliberativa in (molto) breve

La democrazia deliberativa è una *teoria* ed un *progetto politico*. Come *teoria*, la democrazia deliberativa mette al centro la discussione, il rispetto reciproco tra le parti, la parità di trattamento, l'inclusione e la consequenzialità delle decisioni prese. In un sistema democratico ben funzionante, la sfera pubblica è il fulcro delle idee politiche. Da qui vengono formulate nuove richieste, che vengono trasmesse alla sfera del potere, ovvero il luogo delle decisioni. Tra la sfera pubblica e quella del potere esiste una relazione stretta di trasmissione e gestione delle idee.[1] Come *progetto politico*, la democrazia deliberativa offre ai cittadini la possibilità di partecipare alle decisioni politiche attraverso pratiche deliberative che prendono la forma di assemblee di cittadini scelti in modo

1 Dryzek, J.S., 2010. Foundations and Frontiers of Deliberative Governance. Oxford University Press.
Mansbridge J., J. Bohman; S. Chambers; T. Christiano; A. Fung; J. Parkinson; D. F. Thompson; and M. E. Warren. 2012. "A systemic approach to deliberative democracy" in J. Parkinson and J. Mansbridge (eds), Deliberative Systems. Cambridge: Cambridge University Press. Pp. 1–26

casuale. Queste forme di partecipazione democratica sono diffuse in tutto il mondo e sono spesso associate a processi della democrazia rappresentativa o diretta. In Irlanda ad esempio le *Citizens' Assembly* consigliano al parlamento quali leggi dovrebbero essere riviste. In Oregon, le *Citizens' Initiative Reviews* sono incaricate a dare indicazione di voto e scrivere gli opuscoletti informativi che accompagnano i referendum. Oppure, nella regione belga dell'Ostbelgien, il *Permanenter Bürgerdialog* discute tematiche che poi vengono inserite nell'agenda legislativa della regione. Come rimarcato dalle ricerche accademiche, i progetti di democrazia deliberativa sono importanti perché permettono di aumentare la capacità deliberativa della sfera pubblica, ma anche perché danno la possibilità a voci marginalizzate di esprimere le proprie idee e essere ascoltati dal potere politico.[2]

Covid-19 e democrazia deliberativa

Il Covid-19 sta avendo un forte impatto negativo sui vari sistemi politici. Secondo la *Freedom House*[3], il Covid-19 ha deteriorato la qualità democratica di almeno 80 paesi. Conclusioni simili sono state raggiunte dall'istituto *Varieties of Democracy* presso l'Università di Göteborg, che ha rimarcato violazioni delle libertà individuali o abusi di potere ingiustificati da parte delle autorità politiche in gran parte dei paesi del mondo.[4]

---

2 Alnemr N., Choucair T. and & Curato. N. 2020. 2Can the poor exercise deliberative agency in a multimedia saturated society? Lessons from Brazil and Lebanon", Political Research Exchange, 2:1
Nabatchi, T. 2010. "Addressing the Citizenship and Democratic Deficits: The Potential of Deliberative Democracy for Public Administration." The American Review of Public Administration 40 (4): 376–399.

3 https://freedomhouse.org/report/special-report/2020/democracy-under-lockdown

4 https://www.v-dem.net/media/filer_public/52/eb/52eb913a-b1ad-4e55-9b4b-3710ff70d1bf/pb_23.pdf

In generale, oltre alle risposte antidemocratiche di alcuni paesi, il Covid-19 ha accresciuto il potere esecutivo di quasi tutti i governi, che per agire in modo efficace e tempestivo, hanno rafforzato la propria capacità decisionale per imporre restrizioni attraverso misure di confinamento, di quarantena, di coprifuoco e di limitazione delle libertà di movimento. Queste misure, sono figlie della tecnocrazia, ovvero di un sistema nel quale le decisioni legislative ed esecutive sono delegate a esperti. Ad esempio, in Australia, e precisamente nello stato di Victoria, il governo ha imposto uno dei più lunghi e severi lockdown a livello globale. Per 112 giorni, il premier Dan Andrews, accompagnato dalla sua squadra di epidemiologi, analisti di dati ed esperti di salute, annunciavano settimanalmente nuove restrizioni di movimento, di distanziamento sociale forzato, e la chiusura totale di gran parte delle attività economiche e sociali.[5] Lo scopo di Andrews era di sopprimere totalmente il Covid-19 dalla popolazione. Nei media, il caso australiano è stato considerato un esempio da seguire per sconfiggere il Covid-19. Da un punto di vista politico, però è un emblema della perdita di capacità deliberativa della sfera del potere decisionale. Come in altri casi nel mondo, lo stato di Victoria, ha perso la capacità di ascoltare i bisogni provenienti dalla parte della sfera pubblica che è stata particolarmente colpita dal lockdown, ma soprattutto è stato incapace di considerare le proposte provenienti dalla società civile atte ad evitare i costi economici, sociali e politici delle misure di confinamento. Qui si possono citare la mancanza di attuazione di proposte concrete espresse dalla società civile come test di massa, estesi programmi di tracciamento o il rafforzamento del sistema

5 Windholz E..2020. "Public health expert: the technocratic takeover of democracy comes at a high price for all of us" Lens: Monash University. https://www.v-dem.net/media/filer_public/52/eb/52eb913a-b1ad-4e55-9b4b-3710ff70d1bf/pb_23.pdf

sanitario per far fronte alle incertezze dei dati legati alla pandemia.[6]

Oltre al livello sistemico, i lockdown hanno anche un effetto negativo sulla dimensione specifica della democrazia deliberativa. In particolare, misure di distanziamento sociale hanno radicalmente trasformato la natura di molti progetti deliberativi che si sono adattati alla nuova realtà sociale considerando luoghi di incontro virtuali, come nel caso della *UK Citizen Assembly* in Gran Bretagna o l'*Oregon Citizens Assembly* negli Stati Uniti. In entrambi i casi le persone sono state chiamate a deliberare su piattaforme virtuali, un processo che però pone delle limitazioni e mette in pericolo la stessa qualità della deliberazione. Infatti, è ben risaputo che la comunicazione non è solo verbale. Una deliberazione online, ad esempio, trascura l'importanza della comunicazione gestuale che permette a maggiore inclusione dei partecipanti con minore capacità comunicativa verbale, oppure marginalizza le parti della società che hanno difficoltà ad accedere ad internet[7]. In altre parole, come spesso rimarcato, la deliberazione online è meno autentica, meno inclusiva e meno efficace di quella fatta di persona.

In conclusione, si potrebbe affermare che la crisi del Covid-19 non è solo crisi sanitaria, economica o sociale. Ma è anche una crisi di identità per i regimi democratici che si ritrovano senza

---

6 Savulescu Julian 2020. "Is lockdown worth the pain? No, it's a sledgehammer and we have better options." The Conversation. https://theconversation.com/is-lockdown-worth-the-pain-no-its-a-sledgehammer-and-we-have-better-options-145555

7 Baek YM, Wojcieszak M, Delli Carpini M. 2011. "Online versus face-to-face deliberation: Who? Why? What? With what effects?" New Media & Society. 14(3): 363-383.
Friess D. Eilders C. 2015. "A Systematic Review of Online Deliberation Research". Policy and Internet. 7(3): 319-339.
Mendonça RF, Ercan S, Asenbaum H. 2020. "More than Words: a Multidimensional Approach to Deliberative Democracy". Political Studies. Online first

l'anima della comunicazione, più sconnessi e meno deliberativi.

– C –

Länderberichte
Rapports par pays
Relazioni sui paesi
Country reports

Länderberichte

Auch wenn alle Länder von der Pandemie betroffen sind, so reagieren sie doch unterschiedlich darauf. Entsprechend unterschiedliche Auswirkungen hat die Pandemie auch auf diese Länder. Die folgenden Beiträge erkunden solche Auswirkungen beispielhaft für einige ausgewählte Länder und Regionen.

Rapports par pays

Même si tous les pays sont touchés par la pandémie, ils réagissent différemment à celle-ci. Par conséquent, la pandémie a eu des répercussions différentes sur ces États. Les contributions suivantes explorent ces répercussions en se concentrant sur quelques États et régions choisis.

Relazioni sui paesi

Anche se tutti gli Stati sono colpiti dalla stessa pandemia, spesso reagiscono in modi diversi. Di conseguenza, la pandemia ha avuto impatti diversi sui vari paesi. I seguenti articoli esplorano l'impatto del Covid-19 su paesi e regioni selezionate a titolo esemplificativo.

Country reports

Even though all countries are affected by the pandemic, they react differently to it. Accordingly, the pandemic has had different impacts on these countries. The following articles explore such impacts by way of example for some selected countries and regions.

16) Unterstützung für die Schwächsten: Die öffentliche Meinung in der Schweiz während der Corona-Pandemie

Flavia Fossati, Carlo Knotz, Mia Gandenberger & Giuliano Bonoli

Die Wichtigkeit der öffentlichen Meinung in einer gut funktionierenden Demokratie ist unbestritten. Gerade in der Schweiz haben Initiativen und Referenden einen entscheidenden und sichtbaren Einfluss auf die Tagespolitik und insbesondere auf die Ausgestaltung von Politikmassnahmen. Es erstaunt daher auch nicht, dass es für die Regierung wichtig ist die öffentliche Meinung zu kennen, damit vor allem diejenigen Massnahmen, die zur Abstimmung kommen, auch mehrheitsfähig sind.

In schwierigen Zeiten oder in Zeiten schnellen Wandels ist es besonders wichtig, die Meinung der Bevölkerung zu zentralen Themen zu kennen, denn nur mit diesem Wissen kann die Politik adäquat auf die Bedürfnisse der Bevölkerung reagieren. Die wissenschaftliche Forschung zeigt, dass ein gutes Funktionieren jeglicher Massnahmen besonders von der gesamtgesellschaftlichen Zustimmung abhängt und bis zu einem gewissen Grad auch verhindert, dass Referenden oder Initiativen dagegen ergriffen werden.

Die Unterstützung von schwächeren Bevölkerungsgruppen ist ein wichtiger Bereich staatlicher Aktivitäten, wie zum Beispiel von arbeitslosen, kranken oder armen Personen. In der Schweiz fliesst ein grosser Teil des öffentlichen Budgets, nämlich rund 26%, in solche Unterstützungsmassnahmen[1].

1 Bundesamt für Statistik (2020) Statistischer Sozialbericht Schweiz 2019, online https://www.bfs.admin.ch/bfs/de/home/statistiken/soziale-sicherheit.assetdetail.9008560.html, abgerufen 277.11.2020.

Was passiert nun mit den öffentlichen Präferenzen bezüglich der Unterstützung von sozial schwächer gestellten Personen, wenn sich die Umstände in einer Gesellschaft – zum Beispiel wie durch eine Pandemie und eine damit einhergehende Wirtschaftskrise - dramatisch ändern? Dieser Frage gehen wir mit einem Vergleich der öffentlichen Meinung zur Frage einer Einführung eines bedingungslosen Grundeinkommens, im Jahre 2016 und 2020, nach.

Am 5. Juni 2016 wurde in der Schweiz über die Einführung eines bedingungsloses Grundeinkommen abgestimmt. Die Initiative forderte die Einführung einer monatlichen Zahlung, die ein menschenwürdiges Dasein für die ganze Bevölkerung erlauben würde. Dabei wurden vom Initiativkomitee, als Anhaltspunkte wie eine Umsetzung aussehen könnte, monatliche Beträge von 2'500.- Schweizer Franken für erwachsene Personen und von 625.- Schweizer Franken für Kinder und Jugendliche genannt.

Am damaligen Abstimmungssonntag wurde die Vorlage, wie Abbildung 1 zeigt, mit einer Stimmbeteiligung von 46.95% und mit einem Durchschnitt von 23.1% Ja-Stimmen deutlich abgelehnt[2]. Die Zustimmung für das bedingungslose Grundeinkommen war speziell in der Deutschschweiz mit rund 20% und im Tessin mit 22%, tiefer als in den vier Kantonen mit Französischer Amtssprache (Genf, Jura, Neuenburg und Waadt), wo die Zustimmung etwas höher, bei rund 30%, lag.

2 Bundeskanzlei (2016) Vorlage Nr. 601, online https://www.bk.admin.ch/ch/d/pore/va/20160605/det601.html, abgerufen 27.11.2020

Abbildung 1: Resultate der Abstimmung «für ein bedingungsloses Grundeinkommen» im Jahr 2016

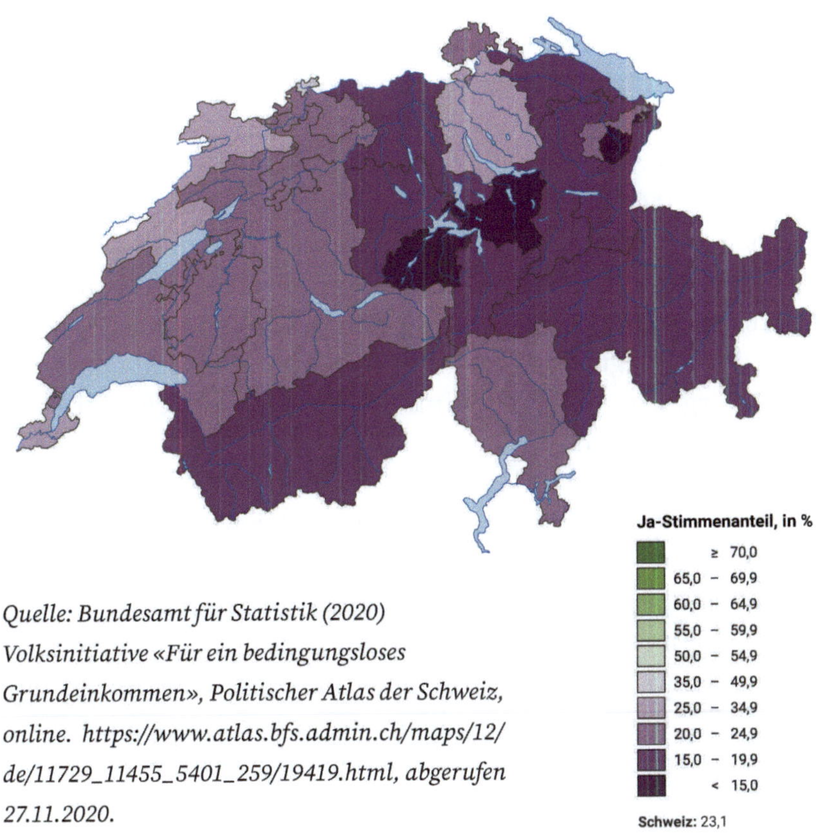

Quelle: Bundesamt für Statistik (2020) Volksinitiative «Für ein bedingungsloses Grundeinkommen», Politischer Atlas der Schweiz, online. https://www.atlas.bfs.admin.ch/maps/12/de/11729_11455_5401_259/19419.html, abgerufen 27.11.2020.

Aus der politikwissenschaftlichen Forschung weiss man, dass eine Veränderung der äusseren Umstände (beispielsweise eine Rezession, steigende Arbeitslosigkeit oder natürliche Katastrophen) einen Einfluss auf die öffentliche Meinung haben können, gerade auch bezüglich der Generosität der staatlichen Unterstützung. Angesichts der grossen ökonomischen und sozialen Herausforderungen und der wachsenden Ungleichheit, die sich während der ersten Pandemiewelle in der Schweiz manifestiert haben, interessierte uns, wie es mit der Zustimmung zu einem bedingungslosen Grundeinkommen steht und, ob dieses an der Urne immer noch verworfen werden würde.

In einer repräsentativen Studie, die auf einer Stichprobe von rund 1500 in der Schweiz wohnhaften Personen basiert, haben wir analysiert, ob die Vorlage von 2016 zur Einführung eines bedingungslosen Grundeinkommens im Frühjahr 2020 immer noch abgelehnt werden würden.[3] Dazu haben wir den Befragten exakt die Frage aus der Abstimmung von 2016 vorgelegt, um die Zustimmungswerte möglichst direkt vergleichen zu können.

Interessanterweise zeigt sich während der ersten Pandemiewelle ein ganz anderes Bild als am Abstimmungssonntag im Jahre 2016. Im April 2020 befürworten im Durchschnitt 63.4% der befragten Personen in der Schweiz ein solches Grundeinkommen. Wie Abbildung 2 zeigt, ist die Zustimmung in den französischsprachigen Regionen dabei mit 72.5% deutlich höher als in den deutschsprachigen Regionen, wo diese lediglich 60% beträgt.

---

3 Die Stichprobe ist ein Abbild der in der Schweiz ansässigen Bevölkerung bezüglich der Merkmale: Alter, Geschlecht, Wohnort (Französisch- oder Deutschsprachiger Bereich) und Bildungsniveau.

Abbildung 2: Zustimmung für ein bedingungsloses Grundeinkommen im April 2019

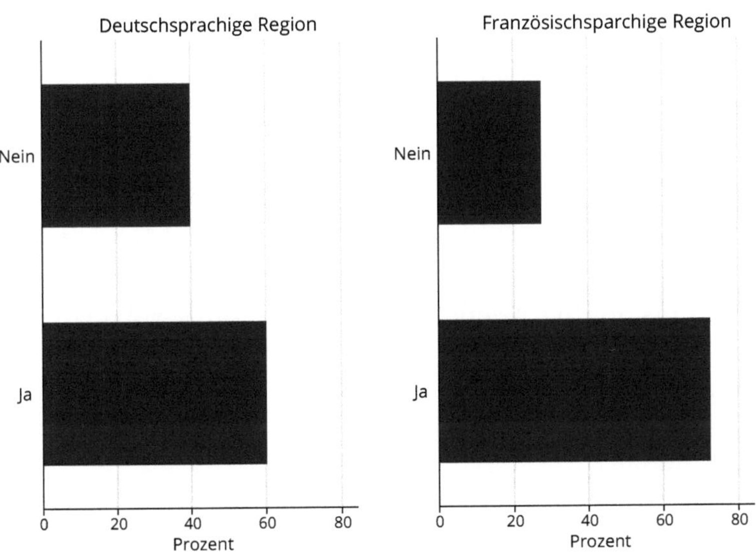

Quelle: Knotz, Carlo, Mia Gandenberger, Philipp Trein, Flavia Fossati and Giuliano Bonoli. 2020. *The IDHEAP/NCCR-on the move survey 'Solidarity in times of crisis' - Data Dashboard*. Lausanne: IDHEAP, Université de Lausanne & NCCR - on the move, online https://idheapunitepolsoc.shinyapps.io/covid_dashboard/, abgerufen 27.11.2020.

Beim Vergleich der beiden Ergebnisse sollte man beachten, dass die Zahlen unterschiedlich «erhoben» wurden: 2016 wurde offiziell abgestimmt, wir haben dagegen nur eine online Umfrage durchgeführt. Das heisst die zwei Resultate sind nur bedingt vergleichbar. Dabei gibt es verschiedene Punkte zu beachten: Über das Referendum im Jahre 2016 wurde nach einer angeregten öffentlichen Debatte abgestimmt, welche es der Bevölkerung erlaubte sich eine fundierte

Meinung zu diesem Thema zu bilden. Ausserdem war bei unserer Umfrage vielleicht nicht allen Befragten klar, dass ein Grundeinkommen gegebenenfalls mit Steuererhöhungen finanziert werden muss.[4] Das heisst in unserer Befragung war eventuell nicht jeder befragten Person gegenwärtig, dass staatliche Unterstützung auch erhebliche Kosten verursachen kann und ein Annehmen der Initiative auch andere reelle Konsequenzen haben würde. Schliesslich, da die Stimmbeteiligung im Jahre 2016 nur gerade rund 47% betrug ist, es auch sehr wahrscheinlich, dass die Abstimmenden eine nicht repräsentative Abbildung der Schweizer Bevölkerung darstellte, wie es hingegen in unserer Befragung der Fall war. Alle diese Faktoren können die Unterschiede zwischen den Resultaten der Jahre 2016 und 2020 wahrscheinlich zumindest teilweise erklären.

Allerdings, und wenngleich man die zwei Resultate nicht direkt vergleichen kann, ist die Abweichung trotz allem sehr deutlich und daher scheint es uns interessant diese zu diskutieren. Die Unterschiede legen nahe, dass es in der Bevölkerung eine grössere Besorgnis bezüglich der durch die Pandemie steigende Ungleichheit und den ökonomischen und sozialen Problemen gibt als dies noch im Jahre 2016 der Fall war. Anders gesagt, scheint es in wirtschaftlich schwierigen Zeiten in der Schweizer Bevölkerung eine stärkere Befürwortung von Wohlfahrtsstaatlicher Unterstützung und Solidarität mit den Schwächsten in der Gesellschaft zu geben. Dies würde auch den Ergebnissen aus einigen international vergleichenden Studien entsprechen.[5]

---

4 Siehe dazu auch das Interview der Politikphilosophin Katja Gentinetta mit dem Schweizer Rundfunk vom 30. November 2020 (https://www.srf.ch/news/schweiz/chancenlose-initiativen-politikphilosophin-was-gratis-ist-muss-irgendjemand-bezahlen; letzter Zugriff am 1. Dezember 2020).

5 Blekesaune, M. (2007). Economic conditions and public attitudes to welfare policies. European Sociological Review, 23(3):393–403; Uunk, W. and van Oorschot,

In einer gut funktionierenden Demokratie würde man angesichts dieses Präferenzwandels dann auch erwarten, dass die Politik tatsächlich auf die Krisensituation reagiert und der Forderung nach mehr sozialer Unterstützung nachkommt.

Im schweizerischen Fall hat die Regierung in Reaktion auf die Pandemie zwar kein bedingungsloses Grundeinkommen eingeführt, allerdings wurden sehr weitreichende Unterstützungsmassnahmen für Personen, Firmen und Sektoren beschlossen, die stärker als andere unter den ökonomischen Folgen der Gesundheitssituation leiden. Manche dieser Subventionen sind sogar nicht weit von der Idee eines bedingungslosen Grundeinkommens entfernt, da sie gar nicht oder nur über sehr lange Zeit zurückbezahlt werden müssen.

Aus diesem Beispiel lässt sich schliessen, dass die schweizerische Regierung durchaus ein Gehör für die sich verändernde öffentliche Meinung und Bedürfnislage hatte und mit entsprechenden Massnahmen reagiert hat. Die spannende Frage wird aber sein, ob die Zustimmung für solche «bedingungslose» Massnahmen auch in «normalen» Zeiten anhalten wird, oder ob sich die Mehrheitsverhältnisse wieder auf das Niveau vom Jahre 2016 einpendeln werden.

W. (2019). Going with the flow? the effect of economic fluctuation on people's solidarity with unemployed people. Social Indicators Research, 143(3):1129–1146. Siehe aber auch bspw. Durr, R. H. (1993). What moves policy sentiment? American Political Science Review, 87(1):158–70.

17) Kompetenz, „Durchregieren“, Deliberation: Covid-19 und die deutsche Demokratie

Dannica Fleuß

Die Covid-19-Pandemie hat weltweit vieles auf die Probe gestellt: die Gesundheitssysteme, Produktions-, Arbeits- und Reisegewohnheiten, die Organisation alltäglicher Besorgungen, die Belastbarkeit der digitalen Infrastruktur und in vielen Fällen auch soziale Beziehungen und persönliche Bewältigungsstrategien. Durch die Pandemie wurde aber auch die *Legitimationsbasis* demokratischer Politik einem Stresstest ausgesetzt: Demokratische Politik ist, so eine Kernintuition, nur dann legitim, wenn sie *vom Volk* (oder seinen RepräsentantInnen) *für das Volk* gemacht wird. Die Covid-19-Pandemie hat jedoch auch etwas verdeutlicht: Insbesondere dann, wenn unter Zeit- und Handlungsdruck Entscheidungen über komplexe politische Fragen getroffen werden müssen, können auch andere Legitimitäts-Faktoren in den Fokus rücken. Inwiefern sind politische Entscheidungen in der Lage, alle relevanten (und bislang bekannten) Fakten, wissenschaftliche Analysen und Prognosen angemessen zu berücksichtigen? Wie können Entscheidungen zum Beispiel über Maskenpflicht und Abstandsregelungen, Kontaktbeschränkungen und Schulschließungen so getroffen werden, dass sie *rechtzeitig* auf das Infektionsgeschehen reagieren? Hiermit rücken gewisse Qualitäten politischer Systeme – also „Kompetenz“, „wissenschaftliche Expertise“ und „Handlungsfähigkeit“ – in den Fokus, die mit den Prinzipien demokratischer Legitimation auch im Konflikt stehen können. Was passiert, wenn Parlamente schlicht zu langsam oder zu wenig kompetent zu sein scheinen, um über anstehende Entscheidungen zu debattieren und zu beschließen? Unter welchen Bedingungen, in welchem Umfang und wie lange kann eine Entmachtung des Parlamentes und ein „Durchregieren“ der Exekutive gerechtfertigt werden?

Mit diesem Stresstest waren in den vergangen Monaten Demokratien weltweit konfrontiert. Die bundesdeutsche Politik hat ihn, so zumindest eine weitverbreitete Einschätzung gerade in der ersten Covid-19-Welle, beispielhaft gemeistert. Das Infektionsgeschehen blieb verhältnismäßig moderat, das Gesundheitssystem konnte an den meisten Orten mit hinreichenden Kapazitäten reagieren und beispielsweise Intensivpflegebetten bereitstellen. Trotz weitreichender Beschränkungen von Freiheitsrechten seit März 2020 ist die Zustimmung der Bevölkerung zur Politik der Bundesregierung in 2020 stark gestiegen. Während im März circa 60% der Befragten der Aussage zustimmten, die Bundesregierung mache ihre Arbeit „eher gut“, gilt dies im November für über 80% (und derzeit immer noch für knapp 80%) der Befragten.[1] Sowohl Angela Merkels inhaltliche Politik – die rasche und konsequente Reaktion auf das Infektionsgeschehen – als auch ihre sachliche, faktengestützte, vor dem Hintergrund eines Dialoges mit WissenschaftlerInnen stattfindende Kommunikation und Begründung derselben haben in vielen nationalen und internationalen Kommentaren Anerkennung und Bewunderung gefunden.[2]

„Notstandsverordnungen“ und „Ausnahmezustände“ haben in der deutschen Geschichte bekanntermaßen eine besonders heikle Rolle gespielt. Mit den im Grundgesetz getroffenen

1 Siehe die Zahlen des Politbarometers der Forschungsgruppe Wahlen e.V.: https://www.forschungsgruppe.de/Umfragen/Politbarometer/Langzeitentwicklung_-_Themen_im_Ueberblick/Politik_II/#Arb_Reg

2 Siehe unter anderem das vom Guardian geteilte Youtube Video „Angela Merkel uses science background in corona virus explainer”.

Bestimmungen gab es zu Beginn des Jahres keine Basis für die Deklaration eines „Ausnahmezustandes“ und für weitreichende, exekutiv verordnete freiheitseinschränkende Maßnahmen.[3] Das Infektionsschutzgesetz (IfSG) bildet die rechtliche Grundlage für die zwischenzeitlich und aktuell geltenden Verordnungen. Dieses Gesetz wurde am 15. März 2020 in einem parlamentarischen Eilverfahren reformiert und ermöglicht nun dem Parlament die Feststellung „eine[r] epidemiologischen Lage nationaler Tragweite“. In dieser können der Bundesregierung, vor allem dem Bundesgesundheitsminister, und den Landesregierungen weitreichende Kompetenzen übertragen werden.[4] Vor dieser Rechtsgrundlage wurde und wird Politik seit März maßgeblich durch die Exekutive – die Regierungschefs der Länder sowie die Bundesregierung – gemacht.

Wie hat sich die deutsche Demokratie im Laufe des letzten Jahres verändert? Und wie steht es um die Legitimität der getroffenen politischen Entscheidungen? Während ich diese Zeilen schreibe wird in Anbetracht der zweiten Covid-19-Welle über einen zweiten harten Lockdown während der Weihnachtsfeiertage debattiert. Insofern findet diese Bewertung nicht nur auf begrenztem Raum, sondern auch in Anbetracht einer sich kontinuierlich ändernden politischen wie epidemiologischen Lage statt. In der Rückschau auf das vergangene Jahr lassen sich nichtsdestotrotz drei Problembereiche identifizieren:

Entparlamentarisierung: Die Dominanz der (Bundes- und Länder-) Exekutive sowie einen Bedeutungsverlust des Bundestages – eine „Entparlamentarisierung“ des

3 Siehe auch W. Merkel (2020). Who Governs in Deep Crisis? Demoractic Theory 7(2), 1-11, S. 3.

4 S. Marschall, S. (2020): Parlamente in der Krise? Der deutsche Parlamentarismus und die Corona-Pandemie. In APuZ 38/2020.

bundesdeutschen politischen Prozesses – wurde schon vor der Corona-Krise diagnostiziert: „der Parlamentarismus litt [...] bereits vor COVID-19 an ‚Vorerkrankungen'". Pandemiebedingte und andere Notstände sind im Allgemeinen die „Stunde der Exekutive". Gerade im Zuge der teilweisen *Lockerungen* von Einschränkungen im Sommer wurde allerdings deutlich, dass auch unter Einbezug aktueller wissenschaftlicher Studien begründete Maßnahmen nicht „alternativlos" sind. Vielmehr ist es eine *politische Entscheidung,* welchen Berufs- oder Statusgruppen welchen Aktivitäten (wieder) Freiräume zugestanden werden und wer Kompensationsleistungen erhält.

Um sowohl auf Covid-10 regierenden Einschränkungen als auch Kompensationsmaßnahmen Legitimität zu verleihen, bedarf es eines Diskurses, der alle Betroffenen im Vorlauf der Beschlussfassung zu Wort kommen lässt. Zumindest aber sollte das Parlament in den bevorstehenden Monaten aber wieder mehr tun als im Eilverfahren Gesetzesänderungen abzustimmen oder *ex post* die Beschlüsse der Ministerpräsidentenkonferenz und Bundesregierung zu akklamieren.[5]

Demokratischer Diskurs und „diskursive Blasen": Diskurse, die demokratische Legitimität stiften, bedürfen lebhafter, kontroverse Debatten innerhalb und außerhalb des Parlamentes, die im Idealfall zu einem gesellschaftsweiten Austausch über politische Alternativen führen. Debatten, die die derzeitige Regierungspolitik explizit infrage stellen, werden jedoch aktuell von Bewegungen und Gruppen

5 Marschall (2020), s. auch Paul Kirchhof, Entparlamentarisierung der Demokratie? In: A. Kaiser/T. Zittel (Ed.). Demokratietheorie und Demokratieentwicklung, Wiesbaden 2004, S. 359–376.

dominiert, die sich bewusst vom politischen System und der Mehrheitsgesellschaft entkoppeln: Medial omnipräsente Gegner der derzeitigen deutschen Corona-Politik sind beispielsweise Angehörige der Querdenken-Bewegung, die unter anderem Demonstrationen organisiert, auf der neben verschwörungstheoretischem Gedankengut offen rechtsradikale Parolen und rechtsradikale Symbolik verbreitet werden.

Expertokratischer Regierungsstil und Gewöhnungseffekte: Die derzeitige Politik ist durch die Dominanz der Exekutive, auch aber durch eine bislang eher unbekannte Bedeutung von WissenschaftlerInnen in politischen Entscheidungsprozessen gekennzeichnet. Dieser Dialog mit der Wissenschaft war und ist für die Bewältigung der Covid-19 Pandemie entscheidend. Nichtsdestotrotz können auf Basis wissenschaftlicher Fakten weder Verteilungsprobleme gelöst noch kontroverse politische Entscheidungen getroffen werden – hierfür bedarf es des Einbezuges des Demos und/oder seiner VertreterInnen in politischen Verfahren. Die vergleichsweise weitreichende Akzeptanz der Regierungspolitik sorgt derzeit für Regelbefolgung und Stabilität. Dies birgt jedoch auch eine Gefahr: Je länger ein Ausnahmezustand besteht und eine sich über Expertise legitimierende Politik betrieben (und anerkannt) wird, desto eher droht eine Normalisierung expertokratischer Modi politischen Entscheidens. Diese stehen allerdings im Konflikt zu dem demokratischen Grundsatz, allgemeinverbindliche Entscheidungen durch die Teilhabe aller Entscheidungsbetroffener an politischen Verfahren zu realisieren – und können auf lange

Sicht, so Wolfgang Merkels Befürchtung, auch eine neue „Untertanenmentalität" befördern.[6]

Der eigentliche „Stresstest" dürfte der bundesdeutschen Demokratie damit noch bevorstehen: Wann wird es gelingen, zu einem regulären politischen Prozess zurückzukehren, dessen Herzstück parlamentarische wie außerparlamentarische Debatten sind? Welche Folgen wird die Covid-19-Pandemie für BürgerInnen, ihre Einstellungen zu Politik und politischer Beteiligung haben – wie wird, kurzgefasst, das „new normal" bundesdeutscher demokratischer Politik aussehen?

6 Siehe kritisch den Podcast „Corona – Gesetzgebung im Eilverfahren" von Mehr Demokratie e.v. (24.11.2020): https://www.mehr-demokratie.de/news/voll/corona-gesetzgebung-im-eilverfahren/

18) Democrazia italiana nello scenario post-pandemico: fra tecnocrazia e populismo

Luca Manucci

Il 31 gennaio 2021 sarà il compleanno dello stato d'emergenza, dichiarato esattamente un anno prima del presidente del consiglio Giuseppe Conte. Alcuni hanno parlato di una democrazia sospesa, dato che la pandemia è stata gestita con una serie di decreti del presidente del consiglio che entrano immediatamente in vigore senza bisogno di essere convertiti in legge. Un regime emergenziale produce decisioni più rapide, e questo può essere un bene quando la situazione è critica, ma un abuso del potere esecutivo potrebbe indebolire il parlamento e il suo ruolo rappresentativo, con conseguenze che potrebbero estendersi anche dopo la fine dell'emergenza sanitaria.

La pandemia, inoltre, ha messo l'Italia di fronte allo specchio, e il paese ha faticato a riconoscersi. Tradizionalmente fieri del proprio sistema sanitario nazionale pubblico, gli italiani si sono accorti che dopo tre decenni all'insegna di austerità, tagli, e "riforme" (in realtà, altri tagli), di quel sistema restava ben poco. Il piano anti-pandemia non veniva aggiornato dal 2016, i letti in terapia intensiva erano troppo pochi, il personale insufficiente. La Lombardia, la regione più colpita, ha reso palese un altro scandalo: la gestione della sanità privata aveva fallito, dato che le privatizzazioni avevano indebolito un sistema sanitario che si definiva d'eccellenza, e che invece è stato letteralmente travolto dall'emergenza.

Il governo formato dal Partito Democratico e dal populista Movimento Cinque Stelle ha spinto non solo per una sospensione della democrazia, applicando norme emergenziali per un periodo estremamente esteso, ma ha anche provato a dare un'immagine di competenza e professionalità che non ha pienamente convinto. Unità di crisi, task force governative, comitati, e virologi ormai star dei salotti TV: se prima si diceva che in Italia ci fossero sessanta milioni di allenatori della nazionale di calcio, ora si può dire che ci siano sessanta milioni di virologi, ma la verità è che nel caos di una informazione senza controlli proliferano le fake news e i complottismi.

Le informazioni fornite hanno fallito nel loro intento di fare chiarezza e rassicurare i cittadini, dato che la loro quantità è stata impossibile da gestire a livello cognitivo e la loro contraddittorietà ha reso l'informazione sul Covid-19 una battaglia politica più che sanitaria. Inoltre, presa dal panico dell'emergenza sanitaria, la classe dirigente italiana ha agito di riflesso, dimostrando la propria arretratezza: gli esperti che il governo ha chiamato per gestire la situazione sono stati in grandissima parte uomini. In particolare, fra i venti membri del comitato tecnico scientifico inizialmente non era presente nemmeno una donna. Più si salgono i gradini della scala del potere, più ci si avvicina ai piani alti della catena decisionale, e meno donne ci sono.

Inizialmente, il governo Conte ha goduto dell'effetto rally 'round the flag, ovvero un aumento improvviso dei consensi per i leader politici in periodi di crisi o guerra, riuscendo a trovare una sintesi delle differenze di vedute in nome di una situazione eccezionale. Conte, inizialmente, era riuscito a rassicurare i cittadini che lo stato stava facendo tutto il possibile per arginare la pandemia, e questo gli aveva permesso di raccogliere oltre il 70% di consensi. Le cose sono cambiate abbastanza velocemente: secondo un sondaggio IPSOS di novembre, il 51% degli intervistati ora ha un giudizio negativo dell'operato del governo per fronteggiare la pandemia, e il 57% dà un giudizio negativo sulle misure di sostegno economico a famiglie e imprese varate dal governo. Dopo una prima ondata vissuta sull'emotività di tante morti inaspettate, l'inno nazionale cantato dai balconi, e l'esplosione di un orgoglio nazionalistico, i cittadini hanno osservato sbigottiti a una seconda ondata che ha trovato il governo completamente impreparato, ancora una volta. E se la fine dell'emergenza sanitaria sembra avvicinarsi con l'arrivo dei vaccini, le conseguenze economiche e sociali di questa crisi lasceranno un cumulo di macerie come già successo con la crisi del 2008.

In questo scenario, le opportunità per la destra populista sono molteplici. Al momento, la Lega di Matteo Salvini e Fratelli d'Italia di Giorgia Meloni volano nei sondaggi: sono il primo e il terzo partito rispettivamente, conquistando insieme quasi il 40% delle intenzioni di voto. Fratelli d'Italia, in particolare, è passato dal 4% ottenuto alle ultime elezioni nazionali nel 2018, ad un consenso che al momento si attesta al 16%, scavalcando addirittura il Movimento Cinque Stelle, che nel 2018 vinse le elezioni con oltre il 32% dei voti. Parte dell'esplosione di Fratelli d'Italia si spiega con una flessione della Lega, che rimane il primo partito con il 23% ma ben lontano dai fasti delle Europee del 2019, quando il partito ottenne il 34% dei consensi.

Il fatto che, se si votasse oggi, il 40% dei voti andrebbe alla destra radicale e populista deve far riflettere su due temi. Primo, il fallimento della sinistra italiana, dato che se si esclude il Partito Democratico il resto della sinistra messo assieme otterrebbe meno dei voti garantiti dal cadavere politico di Berlusconi, che per il solo fatto di mettere il suo nome sul logo di Forza Italia ottiene più consensi di tutta la sinistra radicale. Secondo, la mancanza di credibilità di un partito populista come il Movimento Cinque Stelle, che era stato mandato in parlamento per cambiare la democrazia italiana ma sembra aver fallito su tutta la linea come dimostrato dai sondaggi che al momento danno il partito al 15%, certificando un dimezzamento del suo consenso rispetto a due anni fa. La destra populista d'opposizione di Salvini e Meloni, pur senza aver offerto alcun argomento costruttivo e limitandosi a criticare ogni mossa del governo in maniera opportunista, attrae gli elettori. Il populismo istituzionalizzato dei Cinque Stelle, invece, sembra destinato a scomparire sotto il peso di una situazione drammatica che non si può affrontare solo con "onestà", ma per la quale sono richieste competenze e professionalità.

Se perfino la destra post-fascista incarnata da Giorgia Meloni contesta al governo PD-5Stelle un uso troppo disinvolto ed esteso di misure eccezionali, arrivando a dire che il governo Conte ha distrutto la democrazia italiana, evidentemente qualche problema di legittimità esiste. Non sorprende, in questo senso, che non solo l'estrema destra cavalchi una crisi come quella provocata dalla pandemia, ma che il terreno sia diventato fertile per ogni tipo di teoria del complotto sul Covid-19, da Bill Gates al 5G. In questo senso, bisogna capire un punto essenziale: la rabbia dei gilet arancioni e altri movimenti che vanno dal negazionismo del virus fino a una generica e incoerente critica del governo, intercetta le paure di cittadini confusi, rimasti senza lavoro, e sommersi da informazioni contraddittorie che invece di fare chiarezza rendono il processo decisionale ancora più opaco.

Una volta superata la pandemia, la classe politica italiana dovrà per forza di cose trovare un equilibrio fra la gestione tecnocratica del potere, basata su comitati ed esperti, e la visione populista, che vede nei partiti politici un sistema corrotto, inefficiente, e inaffidabile. Ricucire le divisioni, senza affidarsi a soluzioni semplicistiche. Riconquistare la fiducia dei cittadini, senza instaurare un governo di tecnici custodi della "verità". Solo se si troverà un moto armonico fra i due poli si produrrà una fondamentale fiducia nelle istituzioni, che a sua volta garantirà la sopravvivenza della democrazia rappresentativa.

19) Portugal and the pandemic: Political resilience amid health and economic crisis

Marina Costa Lobo

The Covid-19 pandemic has been a huge challenge for Portugal. On the health side, it is necessary to take into account first and second waves, from January-April and then from October onwards. The trends in Portugal have been moderate to severe, depending on the metric used, and the wave considered. As the health crisis quickly gave way to an economic crisis, successive economic reports by both the OECD[1] and the EU[2] systematically place Portugal as one of the EU countries where the GDP drop is projected to be largest in 2020. The recovery in 2021 is also expected to be slower than EU average. Following on the footsteps of the recent bailout, which ended only 6 years ago, the onset of a renewed crisis falls on a frail economy. Inevitably, these deteriorating social and economic trends had to find a repercussion within the political realm as we will try to explain below. There has been a semblance of democratic normality, amid some worrying institutional trends. Yet, despite indicators of political stress, the political system seems resilient for now.

In Portugal, the Covid-19 pandemic struck just after a newly elected Socialist (PS- Partido Socialista) minority government took office, having won the October 2019 elections. Prime Minister António Costa is not a newcomer. He has been Prime-Minister since 2015 when, following the legislative elections, he assembled a left-wing Socialist minority government with

1 OECD, (2020) Economic Forecast Summary, p.157, OECD: Paris, accessed at https://www.oecd-ilibrary.org/sites/39a88ab1-en/index.html?itemId=/content/publication/39a88ab1-en

2 EC, (2020) Autumn 2020 Economic Forecast, EC: Brussels, pp.31 and 41. Accessed at: https://ec.europa.eu/info/sites/info/files/economy-finance/ip136_en_2.pdf

the parliamentary support of the Communist party (PCP-Partido Comunista Português), and the Left Block (Bloco de Esquerda). Together, the three parties held a majority of seats in the Portuguese Parliament.

Following the 2019 elections, there had been expectations that António Costa would re-enact the Left parliamentary coalition government, or even enter a full-blown coalition with one or both of the Left parties. Despite this, the Prime Minister decided not to enter into any formal agreement, with the Left parties. The PS decided instead to reinforce its pivot role in the political system, negotiating to its left and to its right, with the main opposition party, the centre-right PSD- Partido Social Democrata, depending on the legislation in question. Further reinforcing the idea that the PS can govern beyond left and right, the Prime Minister in May announced that the support for the incumbent President's re-election. Marcelo Rebelo de Sousa, himself a PSD ex-leader, is extremely popular, and polls indicate that he will win with a comfortable majority (around 65% of vote intention) when the election is held in January 2021.

Portugal being a semi-presidential regime, the President has some power to veto legislation, and his legislative powers matter even more when a government has minority status, as is the case with António Costa.

Thus, the 2020 circumstances forged a mutual interest between the two main figures of Portuguese politics: the President and the Prime-Minister. Coming from two opposing parties, in 2020 they depended on each other for their political goals. Namely, the President seeks re-election with a very large majority of votes, and the Prime-Minister seeks government stability.

As a consequence, the two main protagonists of the Portuguese political system have been consensualizing all measures regarding Covid-19, to stem any political crisis that may harm their objectives. Thus, they have been in agreement regarding when to declare the state of emergency, decisions on lockdown, economic decisions regarding furlough as well as other measures. There have been few other parties rejecting the major decisions, both on the left or on the right. Yet, opposition is rising: recently, the government had difficulty in approving the 2020 budget, with the BE actually voting against it, due to the fact that in this party's view it did not dedicate enough funds to combat the economic crisis.

Concerning the functioning of institutions, and democratic procedure, there have been two developments worth noting.

In April, the government decided to transfer 15 million euros to media outlets (radio, newspapers, and television), in the form of paid advertisements. The media has been in crisis for a long time, and the pandemic accelerated a sense of urgency. The government's help however does not bode well for press freedom and independence vis-à-vis the state and government.

Throughout 2020, there has been an attempt to maintain parliamentary activity. Yet, at the same time in August, just before Summer recess, the PS and PSD jointly agreed to end Prime-Minister's bimonthly debates in Parliament. Henceforth, government debates no longer necessitate the presence of the head of government. These debates had been occurring for more than 10 years, and were an occasion for all opposition parties to question the Prime Minister. The growing media visibility which small parties were receiving during the Prime Minister's debates may not have been irrelevant to explain this measure. Both the media funding, as well as the end of PM debates in Parliament point towards the two main parties trying to mitigate the strength of the opposition in the midst of the pandemic.

Thus, institutionally, there has been strategic cooperation, on the part of Portuguese main parties and political actors throughout the 2020 crisis.

Among citizens the consensus seems to be slowly fraying, as Covid-19 progressed in 2020 and the economic crisis started to deepen, but not alarmingly.

There have been occasions where the limitations which the state of emergency produces on rights and freedoms have led to polarized debates on the functioning of democracy in social media. Perhaps where most disagreement has occurred is concerning the organization of large left-wing organizations' celebrations. Thus, the 1st of May celebrations by the Communist-linked Trade Union Confederation- Intersindical, as well as the Communist Party's festival, and in-person Congress were held in 2020 with support from the government, as well as the President. On Facebook and Twitter, polarisation concerning the holding of these events has been rife. Whereas the Left is supportive, the Right has questioned the exceptions allowed for the left organizations to mobilise at a time of maximised restrictions on citizens' everyday life.

To illustrate more generally the trends in citizen attitudes, we will make use of two opinion polls fielded in February and

September 2020[3]. Whereas in February, 75% of the electorate considered the Prime-Minister was responding well to the Covid-19 challenge, this percentage has fallen to 51% in September. The corresponding percentage for the President is 74% and 61%, respectively. When asked about the general government performance, the positive views fell only slightly from 54% in February to 49% in September.

When vote intention is considered, from February to September, the vote intention for the Socialist party actually increased from 33% to 37%, whereas vote intention for the PSD barely moved from 28% to 27%. On the Right, the new entrant - the radical right party Chega - has seen the largest rise in vote intention, moving from 1% to 7%, whereas the conservative CDS-PP which had won 5% in 2019 now seems on the verge of disappearance. The rise of Chega in the polls during 2020 may have fed on the deterioration of confidence in the political authorities' pandemic response, as well as both the President's and the PSD's constant support of the Socialist government's Covid-19 measures.

The rise in vote intention, while large for a new entrant, is still relatively modest, especially considering the disproportionality of the electoral system, but it can be key for future majorities. In the recent regional elections, held in Azores in October 2020, the Socialists lost the regional government, for the first time since 1996, and the PSD decided to form a minority government with right-wing party support from parliament, including Chega. This alliance has not been rejected by PSD leaders for the next legislative elections at the national level.

3 https://sondagens-ics-ul.iscte-iul.pt/wp-content/uploads/2020/10/Sondagem-ICS_ISCTE_Setembro2020_1aparte_final.pdf

Thus, in Portugal, the effect of "rallying around the flag" is in decline, and showing signs of stress. Yet, the main political actors have tended to depoliticize the issue of Covid-19, due to their interests in re-election (President) and government stability (Prime minister). Further, they have cooperated to defuse the populist threat. For now, support for the government and vote intention for the PS still holds. Once the Presidential (re-)election is out of the way in January 2021, and the crisis continues to deepen, the likelihood of de-thawing of the political environment as well as greater polarization will increase.

20) A Loud Constitution and Silent Citizens: Democracy under Covid-19 in Zimbabwe

Daniel Mususa

Democracy requires participation of the citizens, having their views and priorities heard and included when laws and policies governing them are made. In Zimbabwe, democracy is undermined by numerous well documented challenges such as lack of transparency and accountability of the state, unresolved questions of legitimacy that hang above the government despite the holding of successive scheduled elections and human rights violations by the state among other misgivings. The outbreak of Covid-19 as a global pandemic has caused massive shifts in the way the world is run and in how national governments prevent infections and mitigate the impact of the pandemic. Balancing health considerations and respecting human rights and freedoms on the other side is a challenging task which has had adverse impacts on the state of democracy in Zimbabwe. Anecdotal evidence points to the death of democratic deliberation as Covid-19 prevention and mitigation measures are parachuted on the citizens resulting in a very loud and audible constitution but a silent citizenry.

On the 19th of March, the Zimbabwean government declared Covid-19 a national disaster and, through the Public Health Covid-19, Prevention, Containment and Treatment, National Lockdown Order Statutory Instrument (SI) 83 of 2020 (also called the Lockdown Order), announced that the country would begin a 21-day national lockdown. The lockdown order stopped the provision of all services with the exception of activities which the government deemed "essential services." The democratic steps when making legislation in Zimbabwe involve the parliament holding public consultative hearings where Parliamentary Portfolio Committees (PPCs) present the early forms of proposed legislation and elicit feedback from public perceptions. However, the national Covid-19 response showed a departure from democratic principles and went against Zimbabwe's constitution under section 67 (d), which allows for people to *"participate, individually or collectively, in gatherings or groups or in any other manner, in peaceful activities to influence, challenge or support the policies of the Government or any political or whatever cause."* The Statutory Instruments, national lockdown and its related measures were imposed on the nation without any consultation of the citizenry.

The Lockdown Order prohibited private commuter omnibuses from operating, leaving the government-run Zimbabwe United Passenger Company (ZUPCO) as the company allowed to provide public transport services. From Monday the 30th of March—the first working day in the national lockdown—crippling transport shortages were evident. This was exacerbated by the 6PM curfew which people had to observe if they did not want to pay fines specified in the Lockdown Order. The discourse on the lockdown was dominated by a disapproval of the curfew and the crippling decision to have ZUPCO as the lone public transporter. Since the Lockdown Order prohibited any public gatherings, people could not express this disapproval on social media platforms such as WhatsApp, Twitter and Facebook, or openly voice this disapproval in the public bus terminals. Despite it being evident that these measures were adversely impacting a majority of the population, the government did not revise its position on allowing other transport operators to provide services, and neither did it removing or revise the curfew. The state's stance prevailed against the wishes of the people.

The ban on public gatherings was a double-edged sword, which sought to reduce Covid-19 infections but also violated people's democratic rights to assemble and to free movement. The Lockdown Order also issued a blanket ban on movement of people and closure of businesses except those providing "essential services." Subsequent amendments to the Lockdown Order upheld this ban but widened the definition of essential services to include more sectors, but still left out the informal sector which is the main employer in the Zimbabwean economy. People who were caught conducting their informal businesses in high-density residential areas and those attempting to get into town without the travel permits issued by the police were termed "lockdown violators," and subject to arbitrary punishments by the police and army, which was deployed in the main roads and residential areas. They were forced to lie down, or roll on the tarmac, and in many cases they were beaten up by the police and army or forced to do press ups, planks or to perform tough physical tough military exercises called "knees up." The police and army used undue violence and unacceptable measures which violated people's basic rights as enshrined in the country's democratic constitution, for example section 5, which speaks to people's "Right to human dignity," as well as section 52, which speaks to the "Right to personal security."

The main opposition political party members who held a march in Harare protesting against the manner in which the lockdown was being enforced in violation of civil rights were arrested and accused of numerous charges, including "causing public disturbances" and "inciting violence." They were also protesting the violent conduct of the army and police. Despite section 59 of the constitution giving people the democratic right to demonstrate and to petition peacefully, they were charged and arrested. Furthermore, section 87 is explicit on the "Limitations [to these rights] during public emergency," section 87 part 4 (a) does not "*indemnify, or permit or authorise an indemnity for, the State or any institution or agency of the government at any level, or any other person, in respect of any unlawful act*" and part (b) does not "*limit any of the rights referred to in section 86(3), or authorise or permit any of those rights to be violated.*" The constitution is loud and clear on people's rights under democracy, including people's rights to participate in equal and non-coercive deliberation between themselves, and in interaction with the state and its institutions. The new reality is that the pandemic has provided the state with an opportunity to disregard the interests and opinions of the public under the guise of dealing with Covid-19 as a health challenge.

Chapter 17, sections 298 and 299 of the constitution are clear on the expected financial management, principles of public financial management and parliamentary oversight of state revenues and expenditure, and espouses principles of transparency and accountability in financial matters. However, senior government officials including the nation' president's family were implicated in corrupt practices in the procurement and administration of Covid-19 drugs, including donated funds and related equipment for the national response. A prominent journalist who led in breaking the story to the public and was vocal in demanding accountable and transparent use of resources was arrested, paradoxically for corruption, among a concoction of charges including scandalizing the name and office of the president. He was later charged with 'scandalizing' the court that was hearing his matter. His lawyer was disqualified by the court, from representing him because there was a Facebook page running under the lawyer's name, and the court claimed it had no access to the internet so they could (i) not see the page and (ii) verify if indeed the page was created years before, and (iii) is run by some people outside Zimbabwe, and not by the lawyer representing the journalist. Notwithstanding these explanations, the lawyer was removed from representing the journalist.

Effectively, democracy under Covid-19 in Zimbabwe has become devoid of any inclusive deliberation and assessment of competing reasons, framing of arguments or challenges to the state's official position. Contemporary democracy in Zimbabwe under Covid-19 has closed spaces for social movements to participate in dialogue and reflection on key governance discourses such as the financial accountability and conduct of the state. Citizens' participation in democracy beyond elections, citizens' ability to question and assess policies and legislation, is now non-existent. While the constitution is loud and clear on the rights of the citizen and the state's obligations, citizens are now silent, effectively. Covid-19 has provided a veneer for the utter disregard of citizens' rights to speak out on any matters against the government. People can no longer protest or petition on any matter concerning wrongdoing by any arm of the state.

21) Azerbaijan fighting on two fronts: Covid-19 and Nagorno-Karabakh War

Nargiz Hajiyeva

In today's globalized world, the Covid-19 pandemic has affected almost all parts of the world. The pandemic has forced nation-states to boost up their goals of technological innovation, and digital transformation of the fourth industrial revolution. At the same time, in many states it has also uncovered the existing flaws and hitches of their institutions and society.

Response to the Coronavirus Pandemic

Like other countries, the Covid-19 virus did not pass unnoticed in Azerbaijan. Since 24 March 2020, large shopping malls, trade centers, restaurants, cafes have been closed. Metro stations were closed too, and traffic has been restricted due to the strict lockdown imposed by the Government.[1] An Operational Headquarters established under the Cabinet of Ministers due to the Covid-19 pandemic arranged a lockdown-related SMS permission system (8103) when leaving homes during the quarantine, which restricted people's movement by allowing them to go out only once a day for 1 to 3 hours, in cases of essential needs.[2] Until August, even travels were restricted in Azerbaijan's most populous cities, and districts.[3] On March 19, 2020, a Coronavirus Support Fund was established by the Decree of the President. The purpose of the fund is to prevent the spread of coronavirus infection in Azerbaijan and provide

1 Information of the Operational Headquarters under the Cabinet of Ministers of the Republic of Azerbaijan, Available at: https://nk.gov.az/az/article/761/

2 Azerbaijan updates quarantine-related SMS permission system, Available at: https://report.az/en/domestic-politics/azerbaijan-updates-quarantine-related-sms-permission-system/

3 Coronavirus: Access to districts and cities is restricted, Available at: https://www.bbc.com/azeri/azerbaijan-52060075

financial support for measures taken to combat it.[4] To combat Covid-19, activities of the State Agency for Mandatory Health Insurance have been further expanded in the country. Thus, in the current pandemic, its main purpose is to ensure the organization of medical services to protect the health of the population in subordinate medical institutions and to take measures to improve the quality of medical services.

Coronavirus has also affected small and medium-sized businesses in Azerbaijan. Many workplaces were closed and as a result, people lost their jobs. However, the government granted a certain amount of monthly financial assistance, and unemployment benefits were provided to small and medium entrepreneurs[5] as well as unwaged people suffering fromfinancial constraints because of the Covid-19 pandemic.[6][7] Since March 2020, Azerbaijani universities have switched to online education through various programs.[8] Currently, the strict quarantine regime remains in force.

4 Presidential Decree, Rules for the formation, management and use of the Coronavirus Support Fund, Available at: https://president.az/articles/36217

5 Official website of Taxes Ministry of Azerbaijan, Mechanisms of economic growth and state support measures for entrepreneurs, Available at: https://www.taxes.gov.az/az/page/iqtisadi-artima-ve-sahibkarlara-dovlet-desteyi-tedbirlerinin-mexanizmleri

6 How to register as unemployed, who will receive a lump sum payment? - Answer 6 questions, Available at: https://www.bbc.com/azeri/azerbaijan-52208643

7 Official website of Taxes Ministry of Azerbaijan, About the mechanisms of providing financial support to entrepreneurs affected by the coronavirus (COVID-19) pandemic, Available at: https://www.taxes.gov.az/az/post/1020

8 Azerbaijan's experience in fight against coronavirus: Which countries use it? Available at: https://apa.az/en/politics_of_azerbaijan/Azerbaijan's-experience-in-fight-against-coronavirus:-Which-countries-use-it-colorredANALYSIS-color-316949

After the emergence of the Covid-19 pandemic in the country, Azerbaijan realized that...

- the production of new, faster, innovative medical facilities and technologies is crucial;
- more «smart hospitals and healthcare institutions» should have to be built;
- the country has to raise awareness of cutting-edge medical programs including biotechnology, biological medicine, biomedicine, medical engineering, microbiology, etc.

International Assistance to Azerbaijan

In addition to the Coronavirus Support Foundation operating in Azerbaijan during the Covid-19 pandemic, the US Government, through the US Agency for International Development (USAID) and the State Department, has also responded to the economic impact of the Covid-19 in Azerbaijan. An additional 1 million $ has been allocated to the USAID Private Sector Support Project to provide advisory services to the Government of Azerbaijan and technical assistance to small and medium-sized agricultural and agro-tourism enterprises to cope with the pandemic. Moreover, 471'000 $ provided through the State Department will provide shelter, food, and medical and social services to migrants affected by the pandemic. The United States has already allocated more than 5 million $ to support Azerbaijan's response to the immediate and long-term health and economic impact of the Covid-19 pandemic. These funds will be used to provide food and hygiene items to more than 3'600 people in need across the country; educating people about the steps needed to prevent and respond to the spread of the virus; and the successful "REACT-C19" project, which brought 19 doctors from Turkey as consultants to help improve the work of local hospitals. The United States has provided funding to the International Federation of Red Cross and Red Crescent Societies, the International Committee of the Red Cross, the International Organization for Migration, the Azerbaijan Red Crescent Society, and the United Nations Children's Fund (UNICEF) to respond to the Covid-19 pandemic in Azerbaijan.[9] Amid the lockdown, the EU responded to the urgent needs of the Eastern Partnership countries and provided a tailor-made "Covid-19 response package" estimated around 31.6 million € to deliver concrete support to the people of Azerbaijan. The European Union has provided some of the financial support for Covid-19 to provide medical devices, test kits, masks, goggles, safety suits, gowns, and other equipment, and to train medical and laboratory staff, working side by side with the World Health Organization. Presently, the EU continues to support the State Mandatory Health Insurance Agency and "TEBIB" (Management of Medical Territorial Units) to assist the country respond effectually to the Covid-19 pandemic. With the assistance of the EU's Covid-19 package, more than 700 vulnerable families received emergency food and humanitarian aid packages. It also supports online learning for students in Azerbaijan during the Covid-19 pandemic. This online course in design, hairdressing, furniture, and more were developed as part of an EU-funded VET project.[10]

The Impact of both Covid-19 and the War on Politics and Democracy

From the end of September till early November 2020, Azerbaijan was struggling on two different fronts: On the one hand, the country was fighting to cope with the Covid-19

---

9 USAID, Available at: https://www.usaid.gov/az/azerbaijan/press-releases/aug-24-2020-united-states-mobilizes-additional-147-million-respond

10 EU supports online learning for students in Azerbaijan during COVID-19 pandemic, Available at: https://www.euneighbours.eu/en/east/stay-informed/news/eu-supports-online-learning-students-azerbaijan-during-covid-19-pandemic

pandemic, on the other hand, it was involved in the Nagorno-Karabakh war with Armenia. From September 27 to December 12, 2020, martial law was declared in the country due to the commencing of the war. On November 10, 2020, a tripartite deal between Russia, Armenia, and Azerbaijan was signed, including the surrender of several territories from Armenia to Azerbaijan. According to the agreement, a peacekeeping center will be established and Turkish and Russian peacekeeping forces will be stationed in these territories for five years.

It is an undeniable fact that Covid-19 has changed the perspectives of life in the Azerbaijani community. Although parliamentary elections were held in Azerbaijan in early 2020, the Parliament's activity has not been effective due to the impact of the Covid-19 pandemic. Both the first and second wave of Covid-19 have hampered some of the work of the Parliament in the country. Yet, both the pandemic and the war have strengthened political unity in Azerbaijan, increased the importance of diplomacy, and brought international negociations to the center of politics. The double crisis of a pandemic and a war has, as in many other countries, caused a "rally around the flag" effect, with Azerbaijani citizens showing increased support for their political leadership. Especially when it comes to the war, public support for the government has been high: Citizens in different regions of the country took to the streets and chanted slogans by raising national flags in support of the Azerbaijani Army. Moreover, various political parties and organizations operating in the country demonstrated their support for the national leaders, and formed a triangle of "army-political parties-government." Even the opposition party Azerbaijan Popular Front Party (APFP) expressed its political support for the President during the war. In sum, the year 2020 has been a double experience for Azerbaijan, with a war on the one hand and the Covid-19 virus on the other.

22) How Covid-19 is Shaping Georgian Democracy

Zarina Burkadze

The coronavirus pandemic has challenged democracies worldwide. How governments design anti-crisis policies have implications for the quality of democracy. With the high-stakes surrounding democratization, its outbreak increases socio-economic and political uncertainties in Georgia. Amid this unfavorable international context, the war between Azerbaijan and Armenia ignited over the Nagorno-Karabakh region, which is located close to Georgia, ended with a Russian-brokered deal. These changing geopolitical circumstances create additional vulnerabilities for the Georgian import-dependent economy. The government's Covid-19 policies, international assistance, and their implications for democracy are described in this essay.

Response to the Coronavirus Pandemic

Early measures against the nationwide spread of the coronavirus turned effective due to restrictions imposed flight to/from China and Iran. Later, these limitations extended to other coronavirus hotspot states. The Richard G. Lugar Center for Public Health Research immediately started the Covid-19 diagnostic, which is the only Bio Safety Laboratory-3 (BSL-3) in the South Caucasus and Central Asia.[1] On 26 February 2020, the first Covid-19 patient arrived from Iran via Azerbaijan to Georgia. Within weeks, the government announced a nationwide lockdown. Kindergartens, schools and universities switched to online learning. These measures resulted in some disturbing effects. The rights to freedom of movement and assembly were limited and selectively observed. Suspension

1 https://ncdc.ge/Pages/User/LetterContent.aspx?ID=2fd8140d-956a-45a0-bc6c-63f9fdd63346&language=en-US

of public transport and temporary closure of restaurants, shops, and markets worsened socio-economic conditions. For the violation of the State of Emergency provisions (21 March 2020), citizens and legal entities received fines of 3'000 GEL (835 CHF) and 15'000 GEL (4'160 CHF), respectively. For repeated violations, imprisonment of three years was a penalty.

The announcement of national quarantine heavily affected the citizens employed in the private sector and tourism industry. They lost jobs or earned reduced salaries. The government relief package was worth 2 billion GEL (554'545'700 CHF), but the unregistered self-employed workers were not among the beneficiaries. The state subsidized communal taxes and solicited banks to freeze the loan payments for three months. Neither the government nor the banks were transparent that the postponement of loans incurred higher interest rates. Workers did not receive compensation after job cuts that were against the Labor Code of Georgia (Articles 48 and 49). Unemployment and inflation rates increased.[2] Consequently, the prices of food, medicines, and commodities have risen. The government made a one-off payment of 200 GEL (50 CHF) for each citizen under the age of seventeen. Nevertheless, vulnerable groups did not receive adequate support to mitigate the suspension of needed services resulting from lockdown policies.

Doctors and nurses were frontline fighters against the coronavirus, but they lacked healthcare infrastructure and did not have reasonable salaries. Insufficient internet resources limited the effectiveness of online education and the E-court system. The situation remained uneasy for the population of

2 https://www.geostat.ge/ka/single-news/1964/inflatsia-sakartveloshi-2020-tslis-oktomberi

the occupied Abkhazia and Tskhinvali regions. In most cases, the *de facto* authorities denied the patients to receive treatment at the Georgian government-controlled territories, while the Georgian government opened access to Covid-19 related international assistance.[3]

International Assistance

During the pandemic, Russia proactively used misinformation against the Richard G. Lugar Center for Public Health Research to undermine its credibility. Other targets of the misinformation were the EU and US, blamed for inadequate assistance.[4] The EU aided in several stages. Initially, the EU allocated 30 million Euros to provide medical equipment. Small businesses and farmers received 90 million Euros. During the national lockdown, the EU provided Georgia with 183 million Euros to overcome the challenges of the pandemic. When the lockdown ended, the EU additionally mobilized 129 million Euros to support the anti-crisis economic plan. The EU, Sweden, and Austria jointly invested 869'000 Euros in the tourism sector and 1.16 million Euros in organic agriculture. The EU offered an assistance package worth 150 million Euros for macro-financial management.[5] Simultaneously, the United States Agency for International Development (USAID) provided Georgia with 2.7 million USD emergency relief funding and one million USD to enforce preventive measures against the spread of coronavirus. The USAID invested 140 million USD in the Georgian healthcare system during the last two decades, including the Richard G. Lugar Center for Public Health

3 https://www.radiotavisupleba.ge/z/22054

4 https://civil.ge/archives/353894
https://iwpr.net/global-voices/georgia-russias-covid-19-disinformation

5 https://eeas.europa.eu/delegations/georgia/76989/covid-19-team-europe-stands-together-georgia_en

Research, which continues to play a critical role in diagnosing Covid-19 cases.[6]

While Georgia mobilized international assistance, the government did not channel these multifaceted aids adequately. Now, it is difficult to evaluate how the government is using this assistance to manage crises in different sectors of the economy. Conversely, one can easily find system failures in health care. Namely, the government did not create reserves of medicines and ventilators or train specialized doctors. Public hospitals had an insufficient quantity of rapid result testing and PCR tests. The queues at hospitals contributed to the spread of Covid-19. Few private laboratories offered PCR testing at home with a price ranging between 150-200 GEL (40-55 CHF). This service was only accessible for financially able citizens. It is noteworthy that the test-based results are a pre-condition for hospitalization and for receiving online consultation from a personalized doctor. Malfunctioning communication mechanisms between the healthcare agencies and infected citizens additionally aggravated the Covid-19 situation in Georgia.

Implications for Democracy

As Georgia started a gradual re-opening, the coronavirus cases have surged.[7] As a consequence, the pandemic reshaped electoral processes and set new standards for conducting pre-election campaigns. On 31 October 2020, Georgia held the parliamentary elections under a new electoral system with 120 members of parliament proportionally elected in a single nationwide constituency and 30 elected in single-member

6 https://www.usaid.gov/georgia/news-information/news/united-states-provides-1-million-assistance-georgia-respond-covid-19

7 https://stopcov.ge/en

constituencies with a one percent threshold. A transition to a fully-proportional system with a five percent threshold will happen during the next election. These constitutional amendments were a product of the longtime struggle between opposition and government and mediated by Western partners. The challenging part of this election was the reduced number of international observers because of the pandemic.[8] Rallying supporters invariably was problematic for the opposition that asserted that the Central Election Commission committed irregularities. Administration of electoral processes concerning Covid-19 infected and quarantined voters were also burdensome. On 21 November 2020, the eight opposition parties boycotted the run-off elections as the expectations of a coalition government waned. Neither the ruling party nor the opposition is willing to make concessions, which raises issues of legitimacy and effectiveness of the one-party parliament. The difficulties that emerged from the pandemic undermine economic stability, limit fundamental rights such as access to healthcare, education, reshape electoral processes, put vulnerable groups and minorities at greater risk, and skew the field of political competition in favor of incumbents. Georgia is a young and still inexperienced democracy located within a challenging international environment. For this country, Covid-19 is not only a challenge for public health and the economy. Given the pandemic's impact, trust in democracy and its institutions might be at stake.

8 https://www.interpressnews.ge/en/article/109046-ndi-will-not-send-international-observers-to-georgia/
https://agenda.ge/en/news/2020/3255

23) The Impact of Covid-19 on American Politics

Russell J. Dalton

The Covid-19 pandemic has harshly affected the United States. The infection rate and death rates have been substantially higher than most other affluent democracies, the economic impact has been severe, and human suffering continues throughout the nation. What have been the political consequences of the pandemic?

This health care crisis has had a major political impact because the Trump administration and many state governments politicized the crisis. Instead of the unifying message followed by many other democracies, the Trump administration minimized the crisis, did not mobilize national policy, and often dismissed the advice of the health care experts. These actions stimulated the polarization of Americans—there was a Red State story of the crisis and a dramatically different Blue State story. A typical June 2020 Pew Research Poll found that 54 percent of Republicans believed the White House was right in its handling of the crisis, versus only 9 percent of Americans. And then the crisis got worse.

This polarization delayed and deflected government policies on the crisis. It shaped citizens' responses to policies implemented by the state and local governments. Wearing a mask and social distancing became an indicator of one's partisanship—and thus the virus spread. The failures of the national government slowed the development of testing, the production of medical supplies, and treatment—and thus the virus spread. And images of the government's handling of the Covid crisis directly affected the results of the 2020 election and Trump's defeat.

Given these events, are there larger lessons for the democratic process that might flow from this experience? On the one hand, it is too soon to know because the story is still being told and a new administration takes over in 2021.

On the other hand, most observers see that the pandemic highlighted flaws in the system and processes of governance, exacerbated by the policy decisions of the Trump administration. As in most prior political crises, this experience should stimulate efforts to address this democratic deficit.

One positive change already occurred in the administration of elections, which are quite burdensome in the United States. Several states, both red and blue, simplified voter registration or implemented mail-in voting. These reforms contributed to the record turnout in 2020. This experience should encourage many states to continue mail-in voting as the new norm, which expands voter rights and democratic representation. Other potential electoral reforms will likely languish because of the divided party control of Congress.

Other potential institutional reforms might include a reassertion of Congressional powers that have been delegated to the executive branch, greater protection for civil service employees (possibly decreasing the number of political appointments), more stringent regulations on Congressional budget authorizations, and strengthening of Congress's constitutional oversight role. Congress created the Inspector General position in 1978 in reaction to the actions of the Nixon administration; the experience during the Trump administration will generate calls for reform. The pandemic showed the value of federalism in this case, and state politicians may be more active in protecting their sovereignty. These pressures for institutional reform to strengthen democracy will be accompanied by changes in public policy priorities such as additional efforts to provide health care that became so valuable during the pandemic, and policies addressing the issues of economic and social equality.

Finally, many authors have written about the malaise of democratic spirit in America. More likely, many people (especially young people) took democracy for granted. The tumult of the last four years and especially the conflict over declaring a victor in 2020 should rekindle Americans' belief in the importance of democracy.

The caveat to these possibilities is whether polarization will continue at high levels and stymie change of any form. Power is dispersed and divided in the American system. Both sides feel they are in the right, and they both believe that they are the real democrats. Thus reform will require political compromises that have been lacking in recent decades. But if reforms occur, then the pandemic will have produced a stronger and better democratic system.

24) In the Pandemic South America, Science, Polarization, and Limits of Power are in the Center of the Political Debate About Democracy

Jonatas Torresan Marcelino

South America is one of the regions most impacted by Covid-19. Four of the 20 countries[1] with the highest case rates are located in the area: Brazil (3rd), Argentina (10th), Colombia (11th) and Peru (16th). The health emergency hit those countries – which are young democracies with a history of facing political instability during the 20th and 21st centuries – and brought with it consequences that revolve around political polarization, the limits of the separation of powers, and the role of science when public policies are designed and implemented in the South American multicultural societies.

This part of the American continent is very diverse and so are the answers to Covid-19. During the outbreak of the most serious health crisis of the last one hundred years, the presidents of the two biggest economies in the region are playing antagonistic roles. Argentina has 1,5M registered cases and 41k deaths. The country that is governed by Mr. Alberto Fernández, a college professor who sides with the Peronist tradition and follows a very scientific discourse. There, the decisions were taken based on science and a lockdown was imposed throughout 2020. Brazil has 6,9M registered cases and 183k deaths and is governed by Mr. Jair Bolsonaro, a far-right retired captain from the Brazilian Army who openly criticizes scientists and universities. The Brazilian President is not afraid of rejecting the validity of scientific evidence in order to reinforce the political polarization that has been setting

1 Data from the Johns Hopkins University Coronavirus Resource Center, updated on December 16h

the tone of the country's politics since large protests took place in June 2013 and led to the impeachment of President Dilma Rousseff. The protests were the biggest political demonstrations since the redemocratization of the country in 1984. The opposite positions taken by the two most powerful countries in South America when it comes to dealing with the pandemic shows how this region is becoming politically polarized everyday.

Moreover, in Brazil, state governors were responsible for imposing (or not) periods of lockdown and celebrating contracts regarding vaccines while President Bolsonaro harshly criticized lockdown periods and vaccines. He was openly against shutting down the economy, called Covid-19 a "mild flu" (he was later infected with it), and tried to prevent the production of the Chinese vaccine Coronavac in the State of São Paulo. São Paulo is the biggest state in the country, in terms of population and economic power, as it holds 30% of Brazil's GDP. The governor of São Paulo, Mr. João Dória, who is an opposer of Mr. Bolsonaro is also a right wing conservative politician. The debate over the vaccine was taken to the Supreme Court and its ministers had to decide the limits between public health and political polarization. Moreover, the results of the local elections that took place in November points out to a growth among the so called traditional right wing, the center, and the left wing. They all have in common the fact of not being aligned to Bolsonaro.

Making decisions based on scientific evidence did not guarantee any political gain to Mr. Fernández, in Argentina, and Mr. Sebastián Piñera, in Chile. The Argentinian president faced a number of demonstrations organized by the conservatives. They protested against the government and against corruption. The biggest motivator was the controversial decision of removing the judges responsible for the cases involving the Vice-President, Ms. Cristina Kirchner. In Chile, with 576k cases and 15k deaths, the situation is even more acute: After a series of protests that started before the pandemic, the National Parliament finally decided to revoke the country's Constitution, which was still from the period of Augusto Pinochet's regime, cornering a traditional right-wing government.

With the pandemic, liberal sectors also found a voice in Bolivia: After being prevented from running for a third term, Mr. Evo Morales achieved a political victory when his ally in the MAS party, Mr. Luis Arce, was elected president of the country. The party accused the conservative opposition of articulating a coup to prevent Mr. Morales from running, which led the ex-president to go find exile in Argentina even before the pandemic started. After Arce was elected, Morales returned to Bolivia.

Venezuela — a country which is aligned with Mr. Morales and that is under strong economic recession since 2014 — continues to be in the center of the international debate. Mr. Leopoldo López, a conservative politician in opposition to the government and who is in home prison since 2017, took advantage of President Nicolás Maduro's partial amnesty to political opponents to go into exile in Spain. When it comes to the pandemic, the country was less affected than its neighbors with 108k registered cases and 965deaths. Colombia, for example, has 1,4M cases and 39k deaths. After the moderate government of Mr. Juan Manuel Santos, Colombia shifted to the right following the example of its neighbor Brazil and elected Senator Iván Duque as president in 2018. Mr. Duque had to deal with protests against police violence in the country. The serie of protests erupted after the murder of a 46 year old man by two police officers. More deaths occurred as the protests took place.

Located in the Southern border of Colombia, Ecuador faces serious institutional instability during the pandemic. After being blessed by the progressive leader Mr. Rafael Correa, President Lenín Moreno betrayed his political godfather and sided with the conservative wing. Mr. Correa is barred from running for president on charges of corruption. Three vice-presidents have already stepped down from the government. The country registered 202 cases and 13k deaths of Covid-19.

Another of the Andean States that is combining political instability and poor performance in fighting the pandemic is Peru. The country is the fourth largest population in South America (33 million inhabitants) and is reaching the mark of 1M registered cases and 36k deaths. President Martín Vizcarra was removed from office in November after the second process of impeachment took place in the country in three years. He was accused of corruption. Peru underwent violent protests after Mr. Vizcarra was impeached because his approval ratings were high.

Paraguay and Uruguay are currently experiencing a higher level of stability than their neighbors during the pandemic. After a great initial performance, Paraguay has been facing an increase of registered cases during the last weeks. The Paraguayan President Mario Benítez said in May that Brazil was "a great threat" to the local public health. There are now a total of 95k cases and 1,9k deaths. Uruguay, which is currently under the conservative government of Mr. Luis Lacalle Pou after two decades of left-wing presidents, has the lowest rates when compared to any of the countries in this text: 10,4k registered cases and 98 deaths.

The pandemic brought with it a new variable to a region which is known for its institutional instability: the politicization of science that is now added to the political polarization. Moreover, taking into consideration the impact of Covid-19 in the countries, to have a scientific evidence-based approach to politics or to deny those scientific evidences in the name of the economy made little difference. The antipodes Science and Economy can be seen especially in Brazil where the government is inspired mainly by the new populist right headed by Mr. Trump. Pre-pandemic issues – such as corruption and the conservative vs. liberal approaches to violence and social inequality – still remain on the agenda of the country, however. And public health will play a central role in the next elections.

Left-wing and centrist candidates, who were defeated by conservative politicians in elections in Argentina, Brazil, Chile, and Colombia between the years of 2015 and 2018, may have political gains from the pandemic, especially because they are not in power. Nevertheless, any newly elected South American politician will encounter an unprecedented global health and economical crisis without a deadline to end. Under those circumstances, any political victory may be a Pyrrhic victory. The example of Peru demonstrates, more than ever, that victories in elections do not guarantee political stability[2] and governability[3].

2 Reading suggestion: Democracies and dictatorships in Latin America: emergence, survival and fall (Scott Mainwaring, Aníbal Pérez-Liñán). Cambridge University Press, 2014.

3 Reading suggestion: Delegative Democracy? (Guillermo O'Donnell). Helen Kellogg Institute for International Studies, 1993

25) The People's Voices: Congruence Between Japanese Citizens and Their Government During the Covid-19 Crisis

Masakazu Ogami & Masaki Shibutani

1. Introduction

In January 2020, Japan confirmed its first case of Covid-19. On February 25, the Japanese government issued *Basic Policies for Novel Coronavirus Disease Control*, which includes recommendations regarding the temporary closure of schools and workplaces, restrictions on internal movement, and the cancellation of public events.[1] On April 16, 2020, Shinzo Abe, the then-Prime Minister of Japan, declared a nationwide state of emergency and announced a plan to provide a cash handout of 100,000 yen (ca. 870 Swiss francs) as part of an economic stimulus to counter the impacts of Covid-19.[2] Every Japanese citizen who was listed on the country's Basic Resident Register as of April 27, 2020, and foreign residents who carried a visa for more than three months were eligible for the 100,000-yen cash handout. On April 30, the Japanese parliament passed an extra budget for the fiscal year of 2020 that allowed the distribution of cash handouts to all citizens.[3]

1 The Headquarters for Novel Coronavirus Disease Control. 2020. Basic Policies for Novel Coronavirus Disease Control. https://www.mhlw.go.jp/content/10200000/000603610.pdf (accessed December 16, 2020).

2 Satoshi Yamamoto and Maiko Eiraku, "Coronavirus State of Emergency Expanded to All of Japan," NHK World, April 17, 2020. https://www3.nhk.or.jp/nhkworld/en/news/backstories/1036/#:~:text=The%20number%20of%20confirmed%20coronavirus%20infections%20in%20Japan%20exceeded%209%2C000%20on%20Thursday.&text=Abe%20said%20the%20number%20of,the%20state%20of%20emergency%20nationwide (accessed December 5, 2020). The Japanese government has ever hardly given cash handouts to the public before. However, the government distributed a cash handout of 12,000 yen to Japanese citizens in 2009 in response to the global financial crisis triggered by the collapse of Lehman Brothers.

3 "Japan Enacts 25.69 Trillion Yen Extra Budget for Coronavirus Package," Kyodo News, April 30, 2020. https://english.kyodonews.net/news/2020/04/5567e6f46d54-breaking-news-japan-enacts-2569-trillion-yen-extra-budget-for-coronavirus-package.html (accessed December 5, 2020).

In this short article, we shall claim that during the Covid-19 crisis, the issue of congruence between public opinion and policy outcome has become apparent in Japan. After introducing the concept of congruence (Section 2), we argue that Japan's shift in policy occurred so that its policy on cash handouts matched citizens' preferences (Section 3).

2. The Concept of Congruence

The issue of congruence is not exactly new in representative democracies. Indeed, congruence is considered a form of policy representation.[4] Congruence refers to the accordance between the ideologies, attitudes, preferences, and opinions of a country's citizens and those of its political elite—or alternatively, the accordance between the people's wishes and policy outcomes at any given point in time.[5]

The concept of congruence is a matter of degree: The more public opinion and public policy overlap, the more congruent policymaking is. For instance, Patrick Flavin finds that in the United States, policymaking is more congruent with the preferences of high-income citizens than those of low-income citizens.[6]

It has been argued that congruence mostly stems from the results of elections.[7] On this basis, the public elects governments, and the elected governments are expected to create and enact policies that match the public's preferences.

4 Jeffrey R. Lax and Justin H. Philips. "The Democratic Deficit in the States," American Journal of Political Science 56, no. 1 (2012): 148.

5 Daniela Beyer and Miriam Hänni, "Two Sides of the Same Coin? Congruence and Responsiveness as Representative Democracy's Currencies," The Policy Studies Journal 47, no. 1 (2018): 16-7.

6 Patrick Flavin, "Income Inequality and Policy Representation in the American States," American Politics Research 40, no. 1 (2012): 34–44.

7 Beyer and Hänni, "Two Sides," 16.

Yet, as we shall demonstrate, the Japanese government changed its policy on cash handouts to match the majority of the population's preferences, even though there was no election before or after this policy shift.

3. Congruence Between Japanese Citizens and Their Government: The Case of Policymaking Regarding Cash Handouts

The plan of issuing cash handouts to every Japanese citizen regardless of income was announced by Abe after many twists and turns within the ruling Liberal Democratic Party (LDP) and its coalition partner Komeito. On April 7, Abe's Cabinet approved the proposal to provide 300,000 yen (ca. 2,600 Swiss francs) *only* to family households whose income was halved because of the Covid-19 pandemic or to an extent that qualified the household to be exempt from paying residential tax.[8] However, on April 14, Toshihiro Nikai, the LDP secretary-general, proposed a cash handout of 100,000 yen per head to those whose incomes stood below a certain level.[9] Then, on April 15, Komeito Leader Natsuo Yamaguchi held an impromptu meeting with Abe and proposed that 100,000 yen be distributed to every Japanese citizen regardless of income.[10] The following day, Abe announced the plan to distribute cash handouts to Japanese citizens, regardless of income. As a result of this policy shift, the supplementary budget for 2020 through March 2021 was boosted in size from an original 16.81 trillion

8 Satoshi Sugiyama, "Behind the Scenes, an LDP Power Struggle Over Record-Size Economic Package," The Japan Times, April 8, 2020. https://www.japantimes.co.jp/news/2020/04/08/national/politics-diplomacy/ldp-power-struggle-record-economic-aid-package/ (accessed December 5, 2020).

9 "Japan May Pay Out ¥100,000 Per Person to Aid Pandemic-Hit Economy," The Japan Times, April 15, 2020. https://www.japantimes.co.jp/news/2020/04/15/national/government-cash-benefits-may-extend-beyond-head-household/ (accessed December 5, 2020).

10 Naoki Kikuchi et al. "Abe Orders Budget Rewrite to Add 100,000-Yen Handouts to All," The Asahi Shimbun, April 16, 2020. http://www.asahi.com/ajw/articles/13302380 (accessed December 5, 2020).

yen (ca. 150 billion Swiss francs) to 25.69 trillion yen (ca. 220 billion Swiss francs).[11]

It might appear that this policy shift occurred as the government considered the opinions issued by members of the LDP-Komeito ruling coalition, but a question remains: Why did the government finally decide on the distribution of cash handouts to *all* Japanese citizens rather than to only households whose income stood below a certain level? We hold that the influence of public opinion over the policy outcome cannot be ignored.

Table 1 shows the changes in the approval ratings for the government's response to the Covid-19 crisis between February and November 2020 as well as the change in the approval rating for the cash handout policy in April and May 2020. The approval rating for the government's response to the crisis was higher than its disapproval rating in February and March. However, in April, the government received a 50.2% disapproval rating for its handling of the crisis, overtaking the approval rating (46.1%) for the first time. Hence, according to the poll, by April, the majority of Japanese respondents disapproved of the government's response to the coronavirus crisis.

11 "Japan Enacts." To fund the supplementary budget, the Japanese government was set to issue extra government bonds worth 25.69 trillion yen. See Tetsushi Kajimoto, "Japan to Issue Extra Bonds Worth $240 Billion to Fund Coronavirus Stimulus Budget: Draft," April 20, 2020. https://www.reuters.com/article/us-health-coronavirus-japan-bonds-idUSKBN222098 (accessed December 16, 2020).

Table 1. Approval Ratings for Government Actions Taken to Combat the Covid-19 Crisis

Changes in public opinion since the beginning of the Covid-19 crisis			
	Approval	Disapproval	No answer
On the government's response to the Covid-19 crisis			
February, 2020	63.9	30.5	5.7
March	49.3	47.3	3.5
April	46.1	50.2	3.7
May	44.0	52.9	3.2
June	50.9	47.0	2.2
July	49.6	45.7	4.6
August	38.4	58.0	3.7
September	51.6	41.0	7.4
October	54.0	39.7	6.3
November	59.6	34.8	5.7
December	40.5	56.0	3.5
On the distribution of cash handouts			
April, 2020 (before April 16)	43.2	50.0	6.8
May	61.4	26.1	12.5
Source: NHK's monthly poll			

According to that same April poll, the majority of respondents (50%) disapproved of the income-capped 300,000-yen handout program. However, by May, the majority of respondents (61.4%) approved of the universal 100,000-yen handout, regardless of income. Accordingly, the polling suggests that the government's policymaking on cash handouts became more congruent with the majority's preferences in its shift from restricted to universal cash handouts.

We do not deny that other factors affected policymaking, as well. As Figure 1 depicts, approval ratings for the Abe administration declined from February 2020 onwards, and the approval ratings and disapproval ratings for the Abe administration then competed against each other in April. Due to the decreasing trend of approval for the Abe administration, the government might have found it difficult to ignore the majority's preferences. Still, it is fair to say that the issue of congruence between Japanese citizens and their government regarding policymaking on the cash handout appeared during the Covid-19 crisis.

We also think that reaching congruence on specific policy issues with public opinion may not be sufficient to offset declining approval ratings for an administration. Indeed, as Figure 1 shows, after May, approval ratings for the Abe administration never overtook the disapproval ratings until after Abe's resignation. The approval rating for the administration overtook its disapproval rating in September when Yoshihide Suga's new administration took office. Pursuing congruence with public opinion may a necessary step for governments to take to receive support from their citizens, but we leave open the question as to how improving congruence relates to citizens' approval of their government.

Figure 1. Cabinet Approval Ratings
(Source: NHK's Monthly Poll)

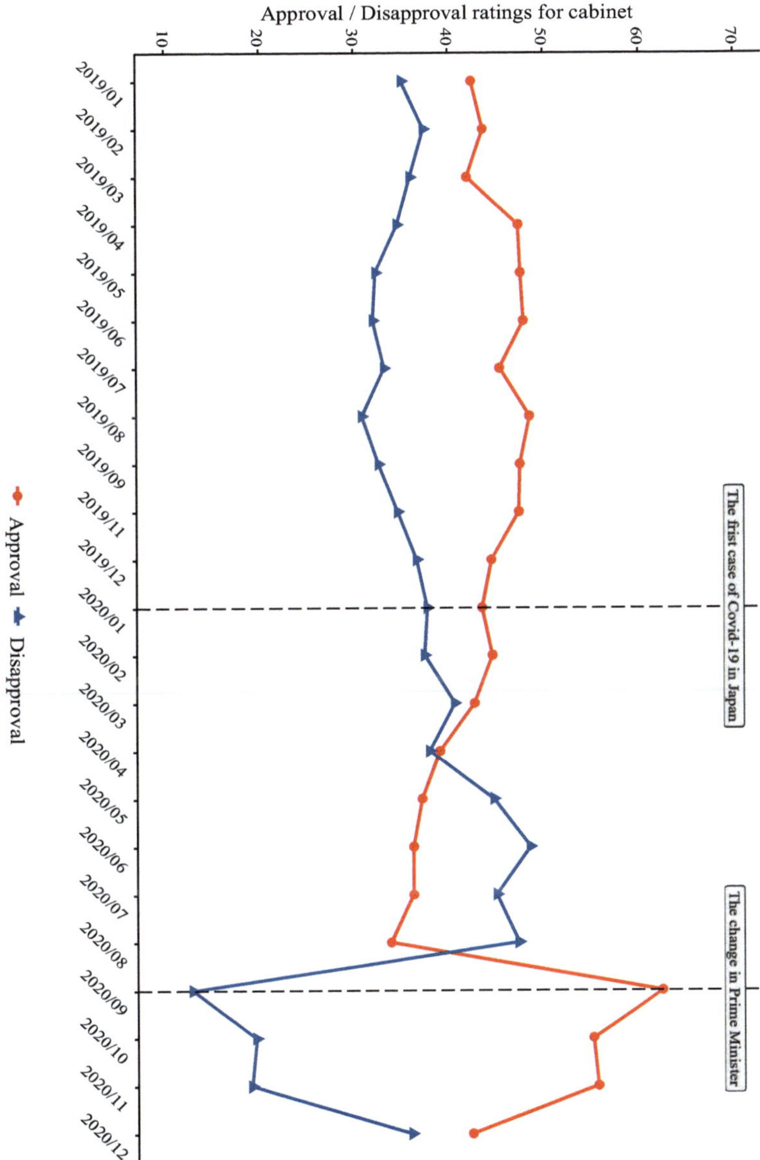

26) How has democracy changed since Covid-19? The Perspective from China

Su Yun Woo

I have to admit that this seems like a peculiar question to ask from the perspective of China but I can imagine that it will be equally interesting to attempt a response that might not do justice to adequately address the complexities that arise in relation to the existing environment in China. To preface this, China is definitely not regarded to be a democracy, quite the contrary in fact, despite having inklings of democracy appearing in unlikely places[1], but mostly susceptible to doubts about its authenticity. Facing allegations of being responsible as the place of origin for the pandemic (disputes still ongoing), China's experience with Covid-19 has been intense in all aspects, with draconian but effective measures to combat the virus. Beyond the focal point of many media reports which centred on the lived experiences of the resilient residents of the epicentre, Wuhan, where the coronavirus was first detected, I had also received first-hand accounts of Chinese and foreign friends living in other parts of the country. They told stories of the human struggle and also of the indomitable spirit, of sacrifice for the sake of the broader community. Talking about sacrifice is very interesting, especially in the context of democratic rights often perceived by some of my Chinese friends, even myself who grew up in a largely non-democratic environment. There is a sense that the emphasis on democratic rights that the Westerners were seen to be

1 Local level village elections were experimented with in China, see for example https://www.mironline.ca/chinas-quiet-experiment-with-democracy/. Deliberative democratic experiments have also been carried out in some parts of China, see https://www.chinafile.com/China-Experiment-Deliberative-Democracy. For a scientific account, see Fishkin, J. S., He, B., Luskin, R. C., & Siu, A. (2010). Deliberative democracy in an unlikely place: Deliberative polling in China. British Journal of Political Science, 40(2), 435-448.

protesting in defence of was misplaced. One or two Chinese friends even told me that this is the downside of democracy in the Western countries in coping with a public health crisis. Most expressed incredulity that democratic rights would take precedence over the public health safety of the community and in juxtaposition to what they see as selfish individualistic behaviour, they also exalted the sacrifice that the Chinese people are making in limiting their own freedom in order to fight the Coronavirus.

The more interesting question that I ask myself was, for China, does Covid-19 make a difference in regards to democracy? Upon further reflection and rumination, I think it does. Given the success of the Chinese government in controlling the spread of the coronavirus and eventually even deemed to have 'eradicated' it (although small outbreaks have happened sporadically after life is purportedly back to normal in China), many Chinese people have lauded the government for its efforts, even if many of these efforts undermined whatever semblance of democratic elements that might have been present. With China's current expertise and prowess in the technological sphere, extending these capabilities to implement effective and extensive contact tracing has stoked fears about the potential for enhancing China's brand of digital authoritarianism which has notoriously manifested in the censorship proclivities, social credit system and surveillance technologies. When the Chinese doctor, Li Wenliang, deemed as the heroic whistle blower who had tried to sound the alarm about the emergence of a new virus that resembled SARS through private post (which went viral) about a medical report, he was taken to task and silenced. A similar curtailing of the already circumscribed freedom of expression can be seen with the ban on a book (Wuhan Diary) by Fang Fang, a Chinese author who had started to record her experiences of the strict lockdown in Wuhan.

So it seems that the actions of the Chinese government in response to the pandemic constituted not only the successful measures to combat and quell the spread of the Coronavirus, but also targeted individuals and caused dire democratic repercussions. In a way, such examples come as no surprise to many since the Chinese government has not exactly been a paragon of democratic virtue, but the exigencies of the current pandemic and the potential dissatisfaction and critiques of the Communist Party regime meant that there will be a heightened sensitivity toward such perceived transgressions. But the cause for concern is rather whether the continuous vigilance in the fight against Covid-19 and the success of the Chinese government will create an acceptance of measures that might further erode any lingering traces of democracy.

Perhaps things may not be so pessimistic and bleak, even in non-democratic China which is in the midst of the pandemic. As much as the pandemic has disrupted local level citizen participatory practices, small pockets of democratic possibilities involving citizen participation using social media still seem to be feasible from what I know from my Chinese collaborators. One of my close collaborators is even able to secure the approval for more test sites for his social media Participatory Budgeting experiments from now to next year since these are taking place online and social distancing is definitely guaranteed[2].

2 https://participedia.net/case/5969

Could this be an unexpected democratic opportunity that emerged out of the Covid-19 crisis? Intriguingly enough, the Chinese word for opportunity and crisis/danger is the same character (机) (ji). But I hesitate to allow myself to let my eternal optimism to run too far and overlook the reality of the current environment in China. Overall, Covid-19 probably connotes more bad news for democratic possibilities in China. As the pandemic continues to assail countries around the world, even if China is fortunate enough to be able to fend off a second wave of infections at the moment, the sense of (potential) crisis lingers. This will mean that some of the measures undertaken in the name of mitigating the pandemic that undermine democratic principles will remain. For me, musing about the question also entails thinking about how perceptions about democracy, as both a political system and idea, changed amongst the ordinary Chinese people. It seems to me that both the success of the Chinese government (despite the earlier blunder with withholding information) and the failure of many democratic countries to prevent the second wave of Covid-19 may incur further scepticism about democracy. This is of course just a conjecture on my part and there is no denying that across the Straits, an excellent example of a democratic Taiwan who had successfully handled the Covid-19 crisis is palpable.

Appendix

Mitwirkende
Collaboratrices & collaborateurs
Collaboratrici & collaboratori
Collaborators

Ammann, Odile **odile.ammann@rwi.uzh.ch**
Odile Ammann, docteure en droit, est maître-assistante en droit public à la Faculté de droit de l'Université de Zurich. Sa thèse d'habilitation porte sur la réglementation du lobbying parlementaire en Europe et aux États-Unis ; ses domaines de recherche sont le droit constitutionnel, le droit international et européen, la théorie du droit et la théorie politique.

Asenbaum, Hans **hans.asenbaum@canberra.edu.au**
Hans Asenbaum is a Postdoctoral Fellow at the Centre for Deliberative Democracy and Global Governance at the University of Canberra and holds a PhD from the University of Westminster. His research interests include identity and inclusion in new participatory spaces, digital politics, and feminist and gender theory.

Bonoli, Guiliano **giuliano.bonoli@unil.ch**
Giuliano Bonoli ist Professor für Sozialpolitik am IDHEAP (Universität Lausanne). Er forscht zu Sozialpolitik, Arbeitsmarkt und Digitalisierung.

Brunner, Palmo **brunner@ipz.uzh.ch**

Palmo Brunner ist Doktorandin und Lehrassistentin am Institut für Politikwissenschaft der Universität Zürich, wo sie in den Bereichen Demokratie, Transnationale Mobilisierung und Diasporapolitik forscht und lehrt. Zudem arbeitet sie als wissenschaftliche Mitarbeiterin an verschiedenen Projekten zum Thema öffentliche Gesundheit.

Burkadze, Zarina **zarina.burkadze@iliauni.edu.ge**

Dr. Zarina Burkadze earned her doctoral degree in political science at the University of Zurich and did her postdoctoral studies at Elliott School of International Affairs, George Washington University. Currently, she is a researcher and lecturer at Ilia State University, Tblisi, Georgia. Her research focus is on democracy promotion and democratization.

Capaul, Raphael **raphael.capaul@rwi.uzh.ch**

Raphael Capaul arbeitet als wissenschaftlicher Mitarbeiter am Zentrum für Rechtsetzungslehre (ZfR) an der Universität Zürich. Seine Forschungsinteressen umfassen Populismus, vergleichende Policy-Analyse und Rechtsetzung.

Caroni, Flavia **caroni@ipz.uzh.ch**

Flavia Caroni ist Doktorandin am Lehrstuhl für Demokratieforschung und Public Governance am Institut für Politikwissenschaft der Universität Zürich. In ihrer Forschung untersucht sie die Mobilisierung im Zusammenhang mit direktdemokratischen Prozessen in der Schweiz.

Dalton, Russell **rdalton@uci.edu**
Russell Dalton is Research Professor at the Center for the Study of Democracy, University of California, Irvine. His research focuses on the role of the citizen in the democratic process and especially electoral politics and participation.

Engler, Sarah **sarah.engler@zda.uzh.ch**
Sarah Engler ist Oberassistentin im Zentrum der Demokratie Aarau und dem Institut für Politikwissenschaft der Universität Zürich. Ihre aktuelle Forschung widmet sich dem Zusammenspiel von Populismus und liberaler Demokratie sowie den politischen Auswirkungen von sozialer Ungleichheit.

Ewert, Christian **christian.ewert@uzh.ch**
Christian Ewert ist Postdoktorand am Zentrum für Demokratie Aarau, Universität Zürich. Er forscht und lehrt zu Regierungsführung, Demokratie und Inhalts- und Diskursanalysen.

Fleuß, Dannica **dannica.fleuss@hsu-hh.de**
Dannica Fleuß ist wissenschaftliche Mitarbeiterin im Bereich Politische Theorie an der Helmut-Schmidt Universität Hamburg und Research Associate am Centre for Deliberative Democracy and Global Governance der University of Canberra (Australien). Ihre Forschung beschäftigt sich mit Demokratietheorie, speziell mit Fragen demokratischer Deliberation und Legitimität, sowie wissenschaftstheoretischen und methodischen Fragen der empirischen Deliberations- und Demokratieforschung.

Fossati, Flavia **flavia.fossati@unil.ch**
Flavia Fossati ist Assistenzprofessorin für Ungleichheit und Integrationsforschung am IDHEAP (Universität Lausanne). Sie forscht zu sozialer Ungleichheit, Sozial- und Arbeitsmarktpolitik und Migration.

Gandenberger, Mia **miakatharina.gandenberger@unil.ch**
Mia Gandenberger ist SNF Doktorierende am IDHEAP (Universität Lausanne). Sie forscht zu Sozialpolitik, politischen Einstellungen und Migration.

Hajiyeva, Nargiz **nargiz_hajiyeva@unec.edu.az**
Nargiz Hajiyeva is a PhD candidate and lecturer at the Azerbaijan State University of Economics (UNEC). Her research interests include global political economy, international security and foreign policy, international law, comparative politics, political theories and energy security.

Hedinger, Franziska **franziska.hedinger@fhnw.ch**
Franziska Hedinger doktoriert am Zentrum für Politische Bildung und Geschichtsdidaktik (FHNW). Ihre Forschungsinteressen sind Fragen zur Umsetzung der Politischen Bildung und videobasierte Lehr-Lern-Forschung.

Heyne, Lea **lea.heyne@ics.ulisboa.pt**
Lea Heyne ist Postdoktorantin am Institut für Sozialwissenschaften der Universität Lissabon, und arbeitet dort im ERC Maple Projekt (http://www.maple.ics.ulisboa.pt/). Sie forscht zu Demokratiezufriedenheit, Wahlverhalten, und dem Einfluss der Eurokrise auf politische Einstellungen.

Knotz, Carlo Michael **carlomichael.knotz@unil.ch**
Carlo Knotz ist SNSF Senior Researcher am IDHEAP (Universität Lausanne). Er forscht zur Arbeitsmarkt- und Sozialpolitik, politischen Einstellungen und Migration.

Lobo, Marina Costa **marina.costalobo@ics.ul.pt**
Marina Costa Lobo is a Principal Researcher at the Institute of Social Sciences of the University of Lisbon. Her research interests centre on electoral behaviour in Portugal and the EU, especially concerning short-term effects.

Manucci, Luca **luca.manucci@ics.ulisboa.pt**
Luca Manucci è un ricercatore presso l'Università di Lisbona, dove lavora al progetto "Populus: Rethinking Populism" finanziato dalla Fondazione per la Scienza e la Tecnologia (PDTC/SOC-OC/28524/2017). La sua ricerca si occupa dei legami fra populismo e memoria collettiva, lo studio comparato dei sistemi e partiti politici, della comunicazione politica e della sua mediatizzazione.

Mususa, Daniel **83dmususa@gmail.com**
Daniel Musua is a senior researcher with Manica Youth Assembly, a local NGO in Mutare, Zimbabwe. His research interests are Youth and Active Citizenship, Deliberative Democracy, Community Security, Youth Sexual and Reproductive Health Services.

Ogami, Masakazu **masakazu.ogami@uzh.ch**
Masakazu Ogami is a PhD candidate at the University of Zurich. He works in the area of normative democratic theory and intergenerational justice.

Repetti, Marion **marion.repetti@hevs.ch**
Marion Repetti is the head of the institute of social work at the University of Applied Sciences and Arts of Western Switzerland, HES-SO Valais-Wallis. She has a PhD in social sciences, with a specialisation in sociology. Her research focuses on social policies, ageing, inequalities and migration.

Shibutani, Masaki **shibutani.m.aa@m.titech.ac.jp**
Masaki Shibutani is a PhD candidate at Tokyo Institute of Technology. He works in the area of voting behavior and public opinion.

Torresan Marcelino, Jonatas **jonatas.torresan@gmail.com**
Jonatas Torresan Marcelino is a journalist and holds a PhD in International Relations from the University of São Paulo. His research interests include public opinion, social networks, Brazil, international relations, democracy, and Latin American studies.

Valsangiacomo, Chiara **chiara.valsangiacomo@uzh.ch**
Chiara Valsangiacomo è una dottoranda in scienze politiche presso l'Università di Zurigo. La sua ricerca si concentra sull'ambito della filosofia politica e delle teorie normative della democrazia, con una tesi di dottorato sul tema della democrazia liquida.

Veri, Francesco **francesco.veri@canberra.edu.au**
Dr. Francesco Veri is a Postdoctoral fellow at the Centre for Deliberative Democracy and Global Governance at the University of Canberra (Australia). Francesco is a comparative scholar specialized in the field of deliberative democracy and political methodology.

Woo, Su Yun **suyun.woo@uzh.ch**

SuYun Woo is a postdoctoral researcher at the Institute of Political Science at the University of Zurich. Her research interests include deliberative governance, democratic innovations, China studies, urban governance, Chinese foreign policy, as well as citizen participation.

Zermatten, Maxime G. **maxime.z@hotmail.com**

Maxime Zermatten est médecin assistant dans le Service de médecine interne du Centre hospitalier universitaire vaudois (CHUV) et collaborateur de recherche au Hemostasis and Platelet Research Laboratory (CHUV). Dans ce cadre, il s'intéresse aux troubles de la coagulation sanguine, particulièrement dans la cirrhose hépatique.

Danksagung

Wir möchten uns bei allen DemocracyNet-Mitgliedern für ihre Unterstützung bedanken, insbesondere bei Odile Ammann und Chiara Valsangiacomo für ihre Hilfe bei den Übersetzungen.

Remerciements

Nous tenons à remercier tous les membres de DemocracyNet pour leur soutien, en particulier Odile Ammann et Chiara Valsangiacomo pour leur aide en lien avec les traductions.

Riconoscimenti

Desideriamo ringraziare tutti i membri di DemocracyNet per il loro sostegno, in particolare Odile Ammann e Chiara Valsangiacomo per il loro aiuto nelle traduzioni.

Acknowledgements

We would like to thank all DemocracyNet members for their support, especially Odile Ammann and Chiara Valsangiacomo for their help with the translations.

Lea Heyne & Christian Ewert

DemocracyNet

DemocracyNet ist eine überparteiliche und gemeinnützige Vereinigung von und für Demokratieforschende, die sich der Demokratie aus verschiedenen Disziplinen und Perspektiven nähern. Sie hat ihren Sitz in der Schweiz, hat aber Mitglieder in der ganzen Welt.

DemocracyNet est une association non partisane et à but non lucratif fondée par et pour les chercheuses et chercheurs qui s'intéressent à la démocratie, et qui abordent ce thème sous différents angles et dans des disciplines variées. L'association a son siège en Suisse, mais compte des membres dans le monde entier.

DemocracyNet è un'associazione apartitica e senza scopo di lucro costituita da e per le ricercatrici e i ricercatori di diverse discipline che studiano la democrazia da varie prospettive. L'associazione ha sede in Svizzera e conta membri in tutto il mondo.

DemocracyNet is a non-partisan and non-profit association of and for researchers in democracy studies, who approach democracy from various disciplines and perspectives. It is located in Switzerland but has members around the globe.

https://democracynet.eu